FORGET THE JONESES:

*Proven Financial Strategies for
an Uncommon Life*

Shawn A. Wakefield

Copyright © 2020 Shawn A. Wakefield & WakefieldSoft LLC

All rights reserved

No part of this book may be reproduced, or stored in a retrieval system, or transmitted in any form or by any means, electronic, mechanical, photocopying, recording, or otherwise, without express written permission of the publisher.

ISBN-13: 9798645520991

Printed in the United States of America

This book is dedicated to my lovely wife and my children who are a significant part of my life story. I hope that my financial choices have a positive impact on them and their future families. A special thanks to my wife who is my best friend and partner in this life adventure. Thanks to my parents for demonstrating a frugal yet happy example of life. Thanks to Bob and Micah for editing and making suggestions to improve this book. Thanks to Kalee and Whitley who during conversations in Nicaragua urged and encouraged me to finally get this book finished. Thanks to Bob for those early conversations about debt and paying it off early. Finally and importantly, thanks be to God.

CONTENTS

Title Page	1
Copyright	2
Dedication	3
Foreword	7
Preface	13
	17
Chapter 1 – Introduction	17
Chapter 2 – Goals and Plans	23
Chapter 3 – Budgeting	27
Chapter 4 - Saving and Investing	38
Chapter 5 - Loans and Debt	50
Chapter 6 - Credit Cards	58
Chapter 7 - Large Purchases	63
Chapter 8 - Advice for Couples	77
Chapter 9 - Children and Finances	80
Chapter 10 - Retirement	85
Chapter 11 - Practical Spending Adjustments	91
Chapter 12 - Conclusion	101

FOREWORD

I will never forget the time and place that Shawn received *The Phone Call*. The timing was stunning... the location was highly symbolic... the content of the phone call blew me away. I would think of that phone call many times throughout my life.

Back in the mid 1980's I was an assistant scoutmaster for a Boy Scout Troop that Shawn Wakefield belonged to. I taught the "bicycling" merit badge and, each weekend, several of the boys would gather at my apartment as the starting point for long weekend bike rides.

Shawn, at age 14, wondered why a Mechanical Engineer at the largest petroleum company in Oklahoma lived in a small apartment with little furniture. After one long weekend bike ride, I invited him to hang out for an hour so that I could show him the reason I was living such a frugal life. I was buying a house and a big part of my salary went toward the large monthly payment. I explained how, with an interest rate at 14.5%, only a small portion of my monthly payment went toward the principle. Most of my payment went toward the interest on the loan. Using my computer, I printed the amortization table showing how my projected payments would allow me to be a homeowner in 30 years. The printout was 8 pages long, single spaced.

And then I showed him what would happen to the amortization table if I contributed an extra $50 a month toward the mortgage. Shawn was surprised to see that the life of the loan dropped from 30 years to less than 20 years all because I added an extra $50 to my monthly payment. And then I showed him how I could save over $20,000 over the long term just by putting my $3,000 Christmas bonus toward the mortgage.

Shawn had a "light bulb moment" there in my small apartment. He realized that a small but uncommon decision, the decision to put a few extra dollars into my mortgage each month, would save me over $250,000.

We kept in touch through his college years… through his marriage and through the birth of his 3 children. More years went by and Shawn mentioned that he and Jana were thinking of retiring early. With 3 kids still in a good school district, they did not just want to pick up and begin exploring the world. They wanted to wait for the kids to graduate high school. After Shawn retired early, with Jana's support, Shawn and I decided to spend 2 months on an adventure of our own. We decided to bicycle across the United States.

After 38 days bicycling from the Atlantic towards the Pacific, we had arrived at the Continental Divide. We had 1,800 miles behind us and only 800 miles to go. Reaching the Continental Divide was a hugely symbolic point in the trip. We had worked hard to get to this point… gradually climbing for the last 38 days and it was going to be "all downhill" from here. We knew that, barring some catastrophic event, nothing was going to stop us from reaching the Pacific Ocean.

It was at that point, at the Continental Divide, that Shawn got *The*

Phone Call I first mentioned. When Shawn began speaking, I realized that the call related to his financial life, so I stepped away so he could talk.

After a somewhat short conversation he pushed his bike toward mine and told me "That was a financial advisor. The advisor wanted to set up a meeting so that he could give me advice on my retirement plans. I told him that I had already retired and was, at this moment, at the Continental Divide in New Mexico and heading by bicycle to the Pacific Ocean."

The timing was incredible. Almost miraculously appropriate for what Shawn was doing with his life.

From the age of 14, Shawn has been a financially responsible person. He married Jana during college. She supported his financial decisions and, together, through two decades of good financial habits, they were able to retire early. It was an uphill climb for both of them because they were self-reliant... they didn't inherit... they worked for everything. So, at the age of 44, they retired early. And, Shawn and I (at age 68) began bicycling across the Unites States.

The symbolism of the location and the content of the phone call blew me away. Shawn had spent his married life gradually saving and building and investing and budgeting so that he could get to the point where he could retire. He could financially coast for the rest of his life. For Shawn, "coasting" means that he would continue to save, build, invest, and budget, but he didn't need to show up at work and spend 40 hours a week in an office. He could instead, temporarily with me, get on a bicycle and see the mountains, forests, deserts, and oceans of this great country. And he and Jana could travel the world together.

In this book, Shawn explains the secrets for their success. He may not mention the fact that he married someone who is as level-headed as he is. And he may not mention the excitement that he had at the times when he realized that their early decisions in life were truly paying off. Shawn has a mathematical mind... he does not often show great emotion. But as you read through this book, I hope you will feel the emotional excitement that I had when hearing of his successes. And realize that this excitement... this success... can also be yours if you follow Shawn's suggestions.

He does not ask you to live an austere life or to make great sacrifices. But, in this book, he shows you how, with a few minor modifications in your life, you can achieve financial security.

He also suggests that you put your ego aside and realize that we often confuse "stuff" as success. Does the purchase of a new car give you the feeling of success? Or would you have a better feeling of success knowing that you had enough money (cash, investments, paid-off home) to allow you to have financial comfort for the rest of your lives?

The parallels of our bike journey across the United States, when compared to Shawn's financial journey are very similar. We spent 17 months planning for the bicycle trip. We went East to West so that we could gradually build our strength before we got to the mountains in New Mexico and Arizona. Most people bike from West to East because they think that they could take advantage of the "perceived" tail wind that might make their journey easier. But on this bike ride, as with his life, Shawn took the road less traveled.

I was truly blessed and honored to have made the bicycle journey with him. And I still think of *The Phone Call*... at that point of our trip... with amazement and pride. Amazed at the timing and proud to have also been with Shawn over 30 years ago when he realized that uncommon financial decisions early in life could lead to great financial rewards later in life.

Read this book. It will change your opinion of what "success" really means. This book shows how, by making minor adjustments to your financial planning, you can retire in comfort and happiness.

Bob Reynolds
(Shawn's fine friend and cross-county bicycle partner)

PREFACE

A dizzying array of finance books line the pages of Amazon, other online book websites, and the shelves of nearly every brick and mortar bookstore. Why would this book be any different than another? Why would this book be worth your time? Because, this book is part of my story. It is based on my experience. This book is not an educated guess at what might or should work in your financial life. This book explains what DID work in my life, including lessons learned from those things that did not work so well.

My name is Shawn. I am married with three adult children. I retired from full time employment at the age of 44. That was five years ago. I did not inherit wealth. I did not have a six-figure salary. For many years, my income was the only income for our household. I have not taken financial education courses from the well-known experts. In other words, I am not very different from you or anyone else who may be reading this book right now.

I am also compelled to state clearly that I am a believer in Christ, and I know that not everyone holds similar beliefs. It is relevant here because it impacts my perspective and my values. A way my beliefs have influenced my financial life is tithing, or giving to my church, 10% or more of my income since before I was married. In part, this book details how I was a steward, or managed, the remaining 90% over which I had influence. The strategies in this book will still be useful if you are not a person of faith right now.

I had considered writing a financial strategy book for several years, but I feel more comfortable now that my retirement has lasted for at least five years. It has proved, in various ways, that my principles and choices were effective then and are working still. I have also been asked recently by numerous young adult couples, to discuss financial topics with them. They have been interested in some level of advice from my wife and I, a couple that is now a bit further down the road of life. A goal for this book is to focus my thoughts and to organize the ideas that I want to impart to those young adults in a helpful, relevant, and comprehensive way. But I sincerely hope these ideas and concepts are helpful and beneficial to you. They certainly have been for me and my family.

Shawn Wakefield
April 2020

CHAPTER 1 – INTRODUCTION

It seems that there is not a shortage of financial advice. We are flooded by information from friends, the internet, Facebook, online blogs, television, and many other sources. But what advice is actually wise and what advice is primarily spoken to increase the speaker's wealth? It can be difficult to filter useful information from the noise. Consider these quotes from notable individuals.

> *"Money is a terrible master but an excellent servant." – P.T. Barnum*

> *"If we command our wealth, we shall be rich and free. If our wealth commands us, we are poor indeed." - Edmund Burke*

These express similar ideas about money and wealth, but I also am reminded of another quote that predates both people.

> *"No one can serve two masters. Either you will hate the one and love the other, or you will be devoted to the one and despise the other. You cannot serve both God and money." – Jesus, as recorded in the Bible, Matthew 6:24*

These quotes influence part of my financial philosophy: I must keep money in perspective, and I must work to prevent its being a master or controlling force in my life. My belief is that God owns everything and that I am entrusted with a small portion of money, wealth, and possessions while I am on this Earth. I am not driven to accumulate money or possessions. I am earnestly trying to manage financial matters well. I tend to be more basic and minimalistic, and I try not to buy or purchase things simply to try to impress others around me.

The tendency to purchase or accumulate to impress or keep up with others can develop into a serious issue. The phrase "keeping up with the Joneses" illustrates this inclination that we can be influenced by that trap. Trying to keep up with others around us can be a common action in the people we see and interact with as well as ourselves at times. My challenge is to **Forget the Joneses** and make uncommon choices. If we make the same choices as everyone around us, we will likely see the same results. Uncommon choices can lead to a more fulfilling, less stressful, and uncommon life.

Now that you know a little of my philosophy, I would like to share with you a short version of my financial story. We are all writing a financial story. We may be early in the story, or we may be in the later chapters, but most of us still have time to alter the ending.

My wife and I both graduated from college in the same year. I graduated with an engineering degree and my wife with a math degree. We both worked for a few years, but when our first child arrived, we decided that she would stay home with our son and that we would live off one income. I tried to start saving early and was moderately successful without saving an inordinate amount of my paycheck. My savings rate never exceeded 10% and was 6% for many years.

Those early years of marriage were not financially out of the ordinary. We were giving 10% of our total income to our church (our tithe). We were saving 10% or less of our total income into an employer 401k account, and not doing much else financially that would be considered unusual. We did budget from the beginning of our marriage, so we were able to track our expenses and usually kept our spending less than our income. We only carried a credit card balance if we had forgotten to mail a payment on time. We did not give much thought to retirement in those early years.

A few more years into our journey we found ourselves living in a smaller town. We had built a large house and fell into the temptation of accumulating a significant amount of stuff, mostly stuff we didn't need. This included many collectible items that lived their life in dark boxes and rarely saw the light of day. We had borrowed money to build the house but were attempting to pay it off early. By now I was self-employed and working from home. Our thoughts of retirement were not organized, but we did hope to retire in our late 50s. However, we did not have a well-defined plan for doing so, even though were we now in our mid 30s. We were raising three kids and trying to manage financially with an unorganized approach.

Fast forward nearly 10 years... an amazing turn of events took place in 2012. I personally believe God began to move us in a new direction at that time. After a vacation to Boston during which we discovered a book about more healthy living. The book was titled *The Blood Sugar Solution* and was primarily about healthy eating. But those better and simpler choices began to cause us to think about other areas of life. We felt strongly that we needed to make some significant life changes. We decided to make deliberate choices to downsize our life and move toward a more minimalistic lifestyle. We were not embracing full minimalism, but we began to adopt some ideas from that side of the spectrum. Initially, we sold many possessions that served no purpose in our life. They were simply owned and not used. We also donated many items that were deemed unnecessary for us. The most dramatic lifestyle change involved selling our custom home. We had built that house fully intending to live there the rest of our lives, but we concluded that was not the most beneficial long-term option. The house was now paid off, and we had a significant amount of equity tied up in the house that was not available to use or invest. (Equity is the value of a property less the loans or mortgages against it.) This choice to sell our house, large and built on an acreage, and move into a smaller and much less expensive home in town was the one choice that surprised many of our friends and neighbors the most. My wife and I were both working at a local community college by this time, and this new home was within walking or biking distance of work for us. Without any significant commute to work, we decided to sell two of our vehicles, leaving us with only one car. We even sold this car in order to buy a smaller, less expensive vehicle with better fuel efficiency. I often biked to work on my electric bicycle or walked on nice days.

After making a number of significant lifestyle changes, we began to look seriously at our retirement plans. Downsizing our house and selling many unnecessary possessions resulted in a significant amount of extra funds. We no longer had any debt, and we had increased our savings rate through payroll deductions at work to a high level, perhaps 25% to 30% of our gross income. We soon believed that early retirement was possible. On the heels of this belief, a major deciding factor for me came after attending multiple funerals within a few months' time. In both cases, the person had worked up until social security age (65 or so), and then ended up dying within a year of that time. For these individuals, life had been all work to save for future opportunities that never became a reality. It was impressed upon me that none of us are guaranteed any number of years in life, and I wanted to spend more time with my family in the future rather than working.

So, after much thought, consideration, and prayer, my wife and I both retired from full time employment at the end of 2014. I was 44 years old. This decision provided several new opportunities nearly immediately. In the spring of 2015, I joined a long-time friend (Bob) on a cross country bicycle ride from the east coast to the west coast. We spent 54 days bicycling 2600 miles and it was an amazing experience.[1] Then, about a year later, my daughter and I bicycled from Oklahoma to Canada. We rode 1200 miles in 18 days on that unsupported trip.[2] Both opportunities would likely have been impossible if I had waited until my late 60s to retire. Retiring early with a modest lifestyle was providing enjoyable experiences that helped to validate my earlier financial choices.

I realize that I have left out many details of our deliberate financial planning. I suppose you may have many questions at this point. The following chapters will delve into detail about many topics that we had to work through in this process. But I would like to give a few general suggestions to touch lightly on the significant strategies and financial choices that made a difference for us. These broad statements could be very helpful if you are early in your income-earning life.

First, a critical aspect of our financial life was budgeting and tracking our expenses. Without this work (and it can be work) we would not have been able to control our spending and plan for larger purchases. We felt that this was a vital building block for nearly every other financial approach we employed.

Second, I would recommend strongly to avoid taking on any credit card debt. This is a great temptation, but it can become a demoralizing burden. Interest rates tend to be very high and therefore paying back these balances can be challenging. However, I would not necessarily recommend to not have a credit card, and I will go into more detail on credit cards in a later chapter.

Thirdly, I would encourage anyone to pay off loans and debt early. I know that there are arguments against this based on interest rates, but in general, the mental and emotional improvement from eliminating debt can be very helpful. One of my earliest financial discussions in high school was with an older friend, who showed me an amortization (or loan payment) table and how paying more (extra toward the loan principal or amount borrowed) early could be a significant benefit later. (If you did not read the Forward, more details on this event are available there.)

And finally, I would urge you to save early and often. I will discuss saving and investing in greater detail in another chapter, but here is the main idea: saving early, and allowing that savings to compound (grow with interest) for a longer period of time, can be a great help to future financial well-being. And this savings could also include investing much of the amount after an emergency balance was established. Saving early is much more powerful and beneficial than saving later in life.

So, those are my big four: budgeting, avoiding/eliminating credit card debt, paying off loans early, and saving/investing.

The last topic that I would like to mention before diving in deeper is that my suggestions are just that, suggestions. What has worked for me and my family may or may not work for you. My choices might not be the best choices for you. There are no financial guarantees in life. I do believe most of the strategies I will discuss can apply to nearly everyone, but ultimately, we each must make our own decisions. Take the concepts and ideas that will be of most benefit to you as your write your financial story. So, forget the Joneses and dare to make uncommon life choices.

CHAPTER 2 – GOALS AND PLANS

"To reach a port we must sail – Sail, not tie at anchor. Sail, not drift." – Franklin Roosevelt

"The plans of the diligent lead to profit as surely as haste leads to poverty." – King Solomon, Proverbs 21:15

So, we have decided that we want to make better financial choices and improve our financial situation, but where do we start? As with any new endeavor, it is extremely beneficial to set goals and have plans.

Typically, goals are set first. We may have a goal of getting out of debt early. Or our goal may be to retire sooner than normal, which could be at different ages for different people. A goal may be to purchase a car, or to save for a down payment on a house. There are numerous goals, both personal and financial, to which we aspire. But as with any goal, we must consider how we might accomplish it. What steps need to be taken to reach a particular goal?

Here are several goals, some of which may be your own, that will be discussed extensively in future chapters…

Creating a basic savings or emergency fund
Buying a new or used vehicle

Buying a house or saving for a down payment
Paying off credit card or other debt
Spending less than you earn
Saving for children's college costs
Reducing your overall spending
Saving for retirement

A dictionary definition of a plan is: "a scheme or method of acting, doing, proceeding, making; developed in advance." It is specific, tangible steps that we develop before even beginning our journey toward a goal which will improve our chances of reaching that goal. If we break these steps into small tasks, then it becomes easier to accomplish them. It will likely take discipline. Despite having to make tough or uncommon choices at times, we can be encouraged in continuing to follow the steps in the plan by keeping our eyes focused on the end goal.

The list of goals above are only that - goals. A goal is a worthy desire or aim, but a goal by itself does not provide any information about achieving that goal. We need to identify and develop a scheme or set of steps that will actively move us closer to our goal.

For instance, if I want to take a vacation backpacking in the mountains, that is a goal. In order to achieve this goal, I need to plan specific and reasonable steps. I might first set a time frame or specific date by which I would like to be in the mountains. I would need to determine the costs associated with taking this vacation. If I plan to drive, then I need a map or route providing directions on how to navigate. There are numerous additional details that I could lay out in my plan to increase the likelihood that I will achieve the goal.

Using this concept of driving and directions is useful for drawing a financial parallel that will prepare us for the next chapter. I may desire to reach a destination, but if I do not know my current location, a map will not help to determine my route or directions. With a mapping app on your phone, your current location is just as necessary as the destination in order to navigate from start to end.

Similarly, we need to assess our current financial position or starting point before we can develop detailed, personalized plans. A monthly budget will act as our current location, and we will dive deep into that concept later.

You may not have set many financial goals before. I have developed some helpful exercises below to help you start thinking about goals. These will be useful as we progress forward and discuss budgeting. Use these exercises to see overall financial goals. Details are not necessary yet. Each chapter will have worksheet style exercises to help you make the concepts real and personalized.

Helpful Exercises

Take some time to list financial goals that you may wish to accomplish in the near and long term. The example of retiring early on $40,000 a year may seem unrealistic, but this is possible based on strategies from this book. For other goals you list, try to estimate a cost and include a date by which you would like to achieve that goal.

Goal	Cost or Dollar Amount	Date to Achieve
Retire early (example)	$40,000 per year	Age 55
Buy a vehicle		
Pay off credit card debt		

CHAPTER 3 – BUDGETING

Last chapter, we discussed the advantages of setting goals and the need to develop a plan in order to move toward reaching those goals. This is especially true in the financial realm. If we do not plan, then we will certainly not magically or spontaneously be able to achieve our goals. It will require planning, diligence and discipline if we want to live in a positive financial environment.

And so, as with any long journey, we need a roadmap. As the Gospel According to Luke records: "For which of you, desiring to build a tower, does not first sit down and count the cost, whether he has enough to complete it?" But sometimes even a map won't be able to tell us if a goal is out of reach. George Washington offers some good advice: "We must consult our means rather than our wishes." We may have desires or wishes (goals), but we must look at our means and whether we have enough available to accomplish that goal.

As we established before, our financial starting point will be a budget. The idea of budgeting may conjure a negative image for many. It may bring to mind accounting ledgers and pages of handwritten columns of numeric data. Simply stated, *a budget is an estimate of income and expenses for a time period.* Just as our mapping app will need to know our current location before plotting a route, we will need to know our current financial situation before beginning to plan and make rational spending decisions.

In addition to just knowing our starting point, a budget has many other practical benefits. By budgeting, we can improve our chances of spending less than we earn, and this can prevent us from using credit cards to bridge the gap. A budget can help us account and plan for larger financial goals, such as building an emergency fund or saving for a down payment on a home.

But for this budget to really work for us, we must track, or add up, our income and expenses as well. In my mind, budgeting must include the expense tracking aspect. Creating a budget and tracking expenses simply cannot be separated if the budget process is to be of any substantial value in our personal financial life. When we add the tracking of our expenses, there are additional benefits beyond just having a budget of expected expenses. We begin to look at our *actual* spending compared to our estimate or budget. With information available on our spending, we can begin to make adjustments and changes to our spending habits. This tracking aspect can be as simple as paper and pencil or it can be automated with financial apps that can do most of the data entry work for us.

All this information about budgeting and tracking may sound good, but I know that you may still be wondering how this is practically implemented. It can be a daunting task to begin, but we can break it down into more understandable steps.

First, we will need to create a simple budget. I would recommend that you do this first on paper to keep it simple and allow for fixing mistakes or making changes. Our budget will include information about our income and about our expenses, or money we expect to spend. On the income portion, we need to determine and add up all our monthly income. If your income is not steady, then it may be best to average the income across several months. If you get paid every two weeks, then with 52 weeks in a year, you need to multiply your bi-weekly income by 26 and divide by 12 to calculate your monthly average income.

Here are examples of finding a monthly average income amount for a paycheck that is not received once a month:

$2,000 twice a month:
$2,000 * 2 = $4,000 monthly

$1500 every two weeks:
$1500 * 26 pay periods per year = $39,000 yearly
$39,000 ÷ 12 months = $3,250 monthly

Some people may have several types of income. Here is another example of determining a total monthly income:

Item	Monthly Amount
Monthly salary	$3,400
Rental income	$500
Small side job, averaged	$200
Total Monthly Income	**$4,100**

Once our monthly income is determined, it becomes our total budget amount for income each month. Write this down once it is calculated. This total monthly income number should be the maximum amount that we spend each month in order to stay positive and not overspend. We need to keep this number in mind for use later.

The next portion of building a budget is estimating expenses. This is more complex and will require more work, but it is not extremely difficult. Rather than just picking numbers for our expenses that we wish they would be, I typically start to build a new budget by using the last month of spending. This may not be what I want to spend each month, but it can be used to build the expense portion of the budget for the first time. Using the last month provides a starting point based on past history.

Again, I would encourage you to determine your estimated monthly expenses on paper initially. Starting on paper will eliminate the complexity of learning a software app at the same time. You will need to put together a list of everything that was spent last month. Sources may include credit card statements, receipts (needed for cash purchases), bank statements, pay apps like PayPal, Venmo, Google Pay, and Apple Pay. You may need to login to each of these and download, print, or write down your list of spending. It can help in later budgeting tasks to make a note on this list of expenditures indicating what was purchased.

Here is an example to use as a template to help create your own list of expenses:

Date	Store or Payee	Note	Amount
Nov 1	Corner Gas	Fuel for Honda	$32.43
Nov 3	OG&E	Utilities / Electric	$79.23
Nov 7	Aldi	Groceries	$94.88
Nov 9	First Bank	House payment	$880.50
Nov 12	Insurance One	Car insurance	$93.50
Nov 15	Netflix	Streaming subscription	$9.99

Build a similar list on paper or with a spreadsheet for all the last full month of expenses. This list should be a complete list of all expenses for that month. Once you have a list of all spending for a month, you will need to assign a category to each expense. The budget will use the total amounts for each category. For instance, if all of our expenses in the Groceries category total to $400, then we would list our monthly budget amount for Groceries as $400. Having categories of expenses in our budget allows us to more easily see where our money is going and what areas require the bulk of our resources.

Some of the expense categories I have used or am currently using include:

Autos and Transportation – includes fuel, repairs, tags, tolls, maintenance, could include car insurance

Food and Dining – includes food, groceries, dining out, but you could separate groceries and dining out into two different categories

Gifts and Donations – includes gifts, donations, tithes, charitable giving

Home – includes rent or house payment, home insurance, annual taxes, repairs, association fees

Kids – includes children's clothing, school costs, camps, day care

Medical – includes health insurance, prescriptions, dental, vision, doctor visits, glasses, medicines

Bills and Utilities – includes gas, electric, water, sewer, trash, phone, internet

Miscellaneous – includes miscellaneous household items, cleaning, clothes for him, clothes for her, discretionary spending, one time or unusual expenses, optional expenses

Miscellaneous is one category where some people may need to break out larger amounts into one or more different categories. For an initial set of categories, you can look over your list of expenses for a month and note what category they may fall into. Your number of expense categories that fit your spending will not necessarily be the same as mine or someone else's list of categories.

Here is an example list of expenses with a category assigned:

Date	Store or Payee	Note	Amount	Category
Nov 1	Corner Gas	Fuel for Honda	$32.43	Auto
Nov 3	OG&E	Utilities / Electric	$79.23	Utilities
Nov 7	Aldi	Groceries	$94.88	Food
Nov 9	First Bank	House payment	$880.50	Home
Nov 12	Insurance One	Car insurance	$93.50	Auto
Nov 15	Netflix	Streaming subscription	$9.99	Miscellaneous

Once categories are assigned to each expense, you will need to make a list of the unique categories. This list will be your list of unique expense categories. Then, for each category, add up all of the monthly expenses assigned to that category. The result will be a list of categories and a total amount of expenses per month for that category.

Here is an example list of expenses totaled by category. This list was made using all of the amounts that I spent in a sample month.

Category	Total Spending
Auto & Transport	$590.00
Bills & Utilities	$260.00
Food & Dining	$680.00
Gifts & Donations	$425.00
Medical	$200.00
Kids	$150.00
Miscellaneous	$344.00
Home	$1,101.00
Total	**$3,750.00**

So, our sample total of all expenses for the previous full month is $3,750. Looking back at our total monthly income, it was $4,100 - meaning we had $350 of our income left over, which is a good situation.

Using the previous month's actual numbers as our starting budget results in a budget like the example below. Note that to balance it out, I inserted the extra $350 into the tablet of budget categories as savings.

Budget Category	Monthly Budget
Auto and Transport	$590
Bills and Utilities	$260
Food and Dining	$680
Gifts and Donations	$425
Medical	$200
Kids	$150
Miscellaneous	$344
Home	$1,101
Savings	$350
Total Expenses	**$4,100**
Total Monthly Income	**$4,100**
Difference	**$0**

We now have a monthly estimated budget that is balanced. Balanced means that our total of expenses in the budget for a month equals our total average income in the budget for that month. If your previous month of spending exceeded your income, then you will need to reduce some categories where possible to balance the budget. It is extremely important that our expenses and income balance out. If our total expenses are larger than our total income, then we will spend too much money each month and overspend our account.

If you have extra money that was not spent, then you have some options on what to do with it, or which of your personal goals to tackle first. You could budget that extra money toward savings, paying off debt, paying extra mortgage principal, etc. We will discuss these topics further in future chapters.

Tracking Expenses

Once our monthly budget is established, the next important piece will be to track our income and expenses in detail for each month moving forward. Tracking or keeping a list of expenses is important each month so that we can know what we are spending. We will need to assign a category to each expense using one of our expense categories as purchases are made and then add up the total expenses in each category at the end of each month. This total will be the actual amount of money that we spent for that month.

One option is to track our spending on paper, and then use a calculator to add up each category at the end of the month. Some people do the budget process this way. Another way is to type each expense from our receipts or bank or card statement into a spreadsheet, and then sort and total the spending in each category at the end of each month. Both methods will work but can be very time consuming. Some people become discouraged due to the amount of work involved.

There is an alternate and perhaps easier option for tracking our spending using an app or software. For many years, I have used an app on my computer or phone to build a budget and total my expenses for each month. I will list a few budgeting programs, but the list changes frequently. I would recommend trying one or two apps to see what works for you. You can enter in one month of expenses just to test the program. Most of these programs can connect to your online accounts and automatically download all transactions. This takes much of the work out of tracking and is a huge advantage over manual methods.

Here are a few currently available apps:

Mint – free but with advertisements; phone and web apps; can sync to online accounts; www.mint.com

Every Dollar - free and paid versions ($129)

Quicken – a PC based app; may have phone apps now; one-time cost as of this writing of $35 to $55; can sync to accounts; www.quicken.com

You Need a Budget (YNAB) – may be good for beginners; browser based but has phone apps; the cost was $7 a month as of this writing; www.youneedabudget.com

PocketGuard – free version; Plus version at an additional cost; some advertising; www.pocketguard.com

Mvelopes – digital version of the 'paper envelopes' method of budgeting; has phone apps; syncs to accounts; $6 a month for basic; www.mvelopes.com

I have personally used Quicken and Mint for long periods of time over the last few years. I first used Quicken, but I have now moved to Mint. I like Mint because it has phone apps and a web interface. It is also free, with tolerable advertisements. I would recommend that you try any of these budget apps and see what works best for your situation.

Budget Adjustments

Once your budget is set up and you are entering and tracking every purchase and expense, now what?

After several months of tracking expenses, it may be time to consider possible adjustments to your budget. Perhaps your spending is higher than you would like in one area, or you may want to start saving for a certain financial goal. Here are likely reasons to adjust your spending budget category amounts or your monthly income budget amounts:

If your income grows, then you would need to adjust your budget and account for the extra income, perhaps in additional savings or debt reduction. A lower income would also require a change to your spending.

At the end of a year, I like to review a full year of spending and see if certain categories need to be adjusted. I look at total budget amounts and compare those to actual total spending amounts.

When there is a season of life change, such as a new child, getting married, buying a home, or kids moving out, changes to the budget are often needed. The type of change will depend on your exact situation.

If a large debt is paid off, then the extra money available can be allocated elsewhere, allowing a budget change on the spending side to put the extra funds into another area or saving for a new goal.

The yearly review can be extremely helpful. I total all expenses for each spending category at the end of the year, and then divide by 12. This will give my monthly average spending for the last year, and I can determine if that is expected in the future and adjust a budget category spending amount up or down as needed. Reasons for changes can vary. Perhaps my commute to work has changed or the price of fuel has changed. My insurance cost for a home or vehicles may be different. Maybe I ate out too much and overspent my food budget. I will either need to adjust my budget or change my habits.

The bottom line is that I need to budget and track expenses and income in order to make informed financial decisions about how much I can save, if I can pay off debt, how much I can spend to stay within my income, etc.

Helpful Exercises

1. Take time to go back and list all your expenses for last month. Use paper or a spreadsheet, but enter every expense. You may need to find receipts or retrieve bank or credit card statements. Be sure to list cash spending, as well. Make a note of what the expense was used for, and this will help create and assign your budget categories.

2. Using your list of expenses, add categories to describe or detail each expense, then total all amounts spent in each category to come up with the total spending for each category in that previous full month.

3. Determine all your monthly income for a typical month. You may need to average irregular income or divide annual income out into a monthly figure.

4. Use the total spending in each category for your starting budget amount. Compare your total income to your total spending for that month. If your spending exceeds your income, you will need to reduce one or more budget categories where spending can be reduced. If your income is higher than spending, then allocate the difference into another category, such as savings or extra debt payments.

You now have a starting income and expense budget to use for this month and future months. You may also want to try out some of the budgeting and tracking apps to make this process easier in the future. Congratulations! You have taken a major step forward into getting a handle on your finances. Having a budget, and tracking expenses will allow other financial goals to be realistically pursued.

CHAPTER 4 - SAVING AND INVESTING

I waited to discuss saving and investing until we had covered budgeting for the simple reason that saving requires planning. Once we have a grip on a reasonable budget, we can use that tool to plan for our savings and other goals. Many people, in discussing savings and finances, talk about the idea of paying yourself first. Paying yourself first is the idea of putting back money into savings from your income before you budget for all of the other necessary expenses. With a solid budget plan, we can pay ourselves first (put money into savings) and still cover our monthly expenses properly. Benjamin Franklin supported the idea of saving when he said: "A penny saved is a penny earned." And centuries before Ben, King Solomon in Proverbs advised that "The wise store up choice food and olive oil, but fools gulp theirs down."

Before we get into the details of saving and investing, some people may ask about the differences between the two. Savings is typically considered to be cash in a savings account or other interest-bearing account, such as a Certificate of Deposit (CD). Savings are usually funds held in an easily accessible account with low risk, which often equals a low interest rate. Investing usually refers to money put into stocks, bonds, or other higher risk investment tools, but the return on these funds (similar to the interest earned) can be much higher than cash in a savings account. In a sense, saving is simply low interest investing. The two go hand in hand to accomplish our long-term financial goals. But most people do not save much if anything each month.

According to a Harris Poll on behalf of CareerBuilder.com in 2017:[3]

- Over 25% of workers do not save anything each month
- Over 50% of workers save less than $100 a month
- Over 50% of workers feel like they will always be in debt

With planning and some effort, you can avoid being part of these statistics.

How Much To Save Or Invest

A common question that I have heard is: "How much should I save?" The answer is not the same for everyone, and it depends on how much you earn and what goals you want to accomplish with your savings. A common rule of thumb is to save 10% of your gross income. This 10% amount may be in an employer plan or on your own. However, I am the first to admit that in my early years I did not follow this recommendation. I started out saving about 5% but tried to increase my savings rate during the first five years of my working career to reach that 10% level. In contrast, as I pressed to retire early, we were saving (or really investing by that time) around 30% of our gross income from two incomes for the household.

I think using percentages of your income is the best way to approach selecting a saving and investing rate or amount. For one thing, a fixed dollar amount will be a very different portion of the income for someone with a lower salary compared to a person with a much higher salary. And as your income changes, using a percentage will cause the actual dollar amount to adjust along with it. I have always put away savings monthly rather than annually. In other words, as I was paid each month, I would transfer my budgeted savings or investing amount over to a separate account that was only used to hold my saved money. Using the separate account prevented me from easily tapping into my savings for unnecessary or impulse purchases. You can look at your budget to see how much of your income is not allocated to expenses. This amount could be a starting point for your savings. You could also try to start with 5% of your income, calculate that dollar amount, and see if it is possible to fit that into your budget.

Another method to increase your savings is to take advantage of a raise or salary increase. If I received a raise of 5% from my employer, I would often increase my savings amount by 1 or 2%. I was still able to have more than half of the additional income from the raise available for other spending, but I could also increase my savings rate without seeing any impact on my budget or having to reduce spending elsewhere. It was a financial win-win.

If your employer offers a 401(k) or another plan with a savings match, it is certainly a good idea to save at least enough to receive all the matching amount. A 401(k) is a company-sponsored savings or retirement plan that employees can make contributions to, often using a payroll deduction. For example, at my first full time job, the company would match fifty cents on the dollar for my contributions to my 401(k) account up to 6% of my salary. In other words, if I put in $10 from my paycheck, my employer would put in an extra $5.00 that was essentially free. I made sure that my 401(k) savings amount through the company was at least 6% of my salary. With the extra 3% (fifty cents on the dollar of my 6% amount) match from my employer, I essentially was able to put back 9% of my salary in savings into the 401(k) retirement account.If your employer offers 401(k) matching, I would encourage you to take advantage of the entire match available. It is essentially free money.

Why Save

Now that we have talked about how much a person might save, let's discuss some reasons or goals for saving. One initial reason to save is for an emergency fund. An emergency fund is money kept in a savings or checking account that can be accessed easily if an emergency expense arises. A few younger couples have asked me about emergency funds, so I think it deserves more discussion. To me, a solid amount of money to keep in savings is the emergency fund. Once the emergency fund is established, we can save for other goals or invest. I consider "savings" to be funds that you might need to access to within the next 1 to 5 years. Money that you might need within the next 5 years should not be invested in the stock market, since the stock market is more volatile. Savings should be kept in a bank account or CDs that can be accessed easily and are safe (less risk).

Emergency Funds

Having an accessible emergency fund is an extremely helpful financial strategy. Unforeseen expenses happen from time to time, and having a pool of money that is easily available as or converted to cash, allows you to pull money out to cover those expenses that are not in your budget. This accessible money also helps to avoid using a credit card to pay for an emergency expense. More on credit cards will be covered in a future chapter.

Possible uses for the emergency fund include:

- Major car repairs
- Significant health care expenses
- Major home repairs
- Expenses during unemployment
- Family emergencies

Emergency fund monies are usually in low risk, liquid (easy to access) accounts for emergency or short-term needs. An emergency fund should not be used to purchase large price tag "want" items in order to avoid having to budget for them. Proper locations for emergency funds include checking accounts, savings or money market accounts, and CDs. Many people suggest having a 6-month emergency fund. In other words, take your monthly budget, multiply by 6, and that should be the dollar amount of your emergency fund. This often considers covering a possible unemployment or job layoff period of several months. I would not blindly select this amount. Review your budget to see if some categories could be reduced or eliminated if a true emergency happened. For instance, if I am saving $500 a month, I would not need to have 6 * $500 or $3,000 in an emergency fund to cover that category because that category would be put on hold or not funded during an emergency or time of unemployement. If your monthly budget is $4,000, multiplying by 6 would result in a suggested emergency fund amount of $24,000. This seems excessive to me and may be much more than you would ever need. It is important to at least have a small, $1,000 to $2,000, emergency fund to cover minor emergencies at least. This would be a good starting point and possible short-term goal. However, you may want to have more than that to feel comfortable in case of an emergency or job loss.

If you have two household incomes, then it is unlikely that all your household income would cease at the same time. If you are more established, and have some lower risk investment funds, then those could be called upon in a serious emergency.

If you choose to have a larger 3 to 6-month emergency fund, then it is important to consider where to have the money located. I would recommend keeping a small amount, perhaps 20%, in your checking account for easy access. If it is too tempting to use the money for something besides emergencies, then move it over to a savings, CD, or money market account. The next

40% could be in a higher yielding (higher interest rate) savings or money market account, since checking account interest rates tend to be low or non-existent. Finally, the last 40% could be in shorter term CDs. You could have several 3- or 6-month CDs and stagger maturity dates. If you needed the funds, you could still easily access them. In the case of CDs, you might lose a small amount of interest, but only for the CDs you cash in. In a true emergency, a few dollars of interest lost is a small price to pay to cover a surprise expense and avoid using a credit card, carrying a balance, and paying interest.

Before we leave the topic of saving, I do want to address a question that I was recently asked. A younger single person asked if it was possible to save and pay off debt at the same time. My short answer would be yes, but I should explain. The small $1,000 to $2,000 emergency fund should be a top priority if you do not have that much saved. After that amount is saved, then use the budget process to your advantage. Budget some amount to add to your saving each month, and budget another amount to work on paying off debt. If the debt interest rate is high, like a credit card, then it may be worth reducing savings temporarily and paying even more against the debt. If the debt interest rate is low, then a more balanced split would be reasonable.

Investing

Investing is essentially saving for the long term. As a general rule, money that will not be needed for five or more years can be invested. For many people, myself included, investing often equals saving for retirement. Investing is putting money into riskier options, such as stocks and bonds, rather than in a low interest account. Investing will help you achieve long-term savings goals, such as retirement, because the average long-term return rates are higher. But lower-risk investing, perhaps in bond funds or higher interest CDs, could be used to earn a higher rate of return to save a down payment for a house or vehicle or for a need that might be within the next few years. We invest in higher risk funds in order to grow our investment savings faster over the long term.

For example:

Here is an initial look at possible growth of a higher versus lower risk investment. If we have an extra $200 per month to save or invest, let's look at options for how that money might grow over 20 years.

Saving $200 per month put into 2-year CDs with a return of about 2.1% results in a balance at the end of 20 years of $59,693 ($48,000 put in plus $19,693 in interest).

A CD or Certificate of Deposit is available through banks. Money is deposited for a certain length of time and the consumer agrees to leave that amount in the CD for the full time period.

Investing $200 per month put into a stock index fund with a return of about 7% results in a balance at the end of 20 years of $104,793 or nearly double!

You can calculate these or other numbers yourself, or using other amounts, by finding a Savings Calculator online. There are many to choose from.

I use a 7% stock market annualized return average here since the S&P has averaged 6 to 8%, depending on how it is calculated, over the last 50 years. The S&P, or Standard and Poor's 500, is a stock market index or benchmark that measures the average performance of 500 large companies in the United States. 100-year stock market annualized average return rates are around 10%, but that is a high average number that we may or may not see over the next 30 or 40 years. I have seen one prominent person claim a 12% average stock market return, but I have looked at their math and they are simply not calculating it correctly. Seven percent is a safe, more dependable, and likely average return rate to use.

So, you may have decided that you want to start investing money in a higher return option. But how can we practically do that?

First, you will need to open a stock account, Roth IRA or Traditional IRA account with an investment company. You can invest or buy funds (mutual funds, index funds, bond funds) using money deposited into any of these accounts. Firms that I have personally dealt with or were recommended include Charles Schwab, Fidelity, Vanguard, or TD Ameritrade. I do all my transactions with my financial company online, and that has worked out great for us. Look at each of these companies and see which one is a good fit for you. Also, if you have already started a 401(k) with your employer, your employer may use a firm that would also let you open another investment account. I would encourage you to do it soon and open an account so that you can begin investing to get the most return possible. Earlier is better when it comes to investing.

What To Invest In

Investing is one of the most common topics that I have been asked about. I have personally moved to a strategy that is quite simple. I invest only in stock index funds and bond index funds. You can purchase index funds with any of the above companies I mentioned, even if the fund is at another firm such as a Fidelity or Vanguard index fund. Index funds are funds that are designed to track the performance of a certain market index, and they tend to track it extremely closely. Stock index funds are comprised of stocks in different companies, chosen to mirror one of the stock index benchmarks, such as the S&P 500, Dow, or Nasdaq. Bond index funds are comprised of bonds (loans to companies or municipalities) and have a lower return but are less risky.

Someone may raise the question at this point about whether or not we could beat the market (index) funds if we pick other mutual funds, individual stocks, or use some newsletter or other investment scheme. In my experience – no. Any schemes, systems, mutual funds, or newsletters that I have paid good money for have not beaten the stock market over the long term. They may advertise and even provide great returns for a short period of time, but we need to be concerned with the long term. So, my advice is to invest in index funds and not worry about watching every stock or getting every "tip" from an "expert".

To support this opinion, let's look at mutual funds in general for a minute. There is a bewildering array of mutual funds in all kinds of market sectors. According to SPIVA (S&P Indexes vs Active), only 20% of actively managed mutual funds beat the market over a 5-year span. Even worse, only 8% of actively managed mutual funds beat the market over a 15 year span.[4] So if we are investing for the long term, and choose to put money in an actively managed mutual fund (most of them), rather than a market index fund, there is a 92% chance that we will NOT beat the market over a 15 year term. That research has certainly convinced me to only invest in stock index funds. The market is already volatile in the short term, and I would not want to add the likelihood that I would never beat the stock market average with an actively managed mutual fund. In addition, mutual fund fees tend to be higher than stock index funds. Even when selecting a stock index fund, look closely to find a low fee or no fee index fund. And if I do choose to buy individual stocks and trade them more often, my trade commissions will start to become a factor and will reduce any gains.

I have decided that I need to be a long term, buy and hold investor, which becomes quite easy with stock index funds. I do not have to watch the market ups and downs daily or weekly. To reduce my risk as we get closer to retirement, I can invest in both stock index funds and bond index funds. The bond funds will have a lower return, but will be more stable in the short term as I need to withdraw money. This is where money I might need sooner should be invested.

One other topic I have not mentioned is annuities. Annuities are financial products that offer a fixed income stream after a series of payments or even a one-time lump sum are paid to the company. Often the annuity also offers a life insurance component. I am not a fan of annuities for a few reasons. First, when the annuity tries to be both insurance and an investment vehicle, it is not able to do either of these things well, and in my experience the investment returns are not very good. Also, there is a loss of control, especially on the annuities that you buy into which pay you a fixed amount for the rest of your life.

I also think that paying a financial advisor is not in my best interest. If they are recommending stocks, then they will make more money if I trade more often and pay more fees which might affect what they recommend. They will also make money even if my portfolio is doing poorly. I have seen an advisor recommend products such as annuities to account for a "worst case scenario" which may never happen. I personally feel that a simple investment strategy with index funds is hard to beat.

For instance, I retired in late 2014 with a portfolio and some other small income sources that I was confident would be enough for my needs. I had talked to a financial account manager about my account and some projections, but it was free advice and I had not yet told him about my retirement. In early 2015, my friend Bob and I embarked on a cross country bicycle ride, unsupported, from the Atlantic Ocean to the Pacific Ocean. We had ridden all the way to the Continental Divide in New Mexico, and we stopped for a rest break and a few photos at the Continental Divide. Ironically, while taking a break, my financial account manager called me and asked if we could discuss my portfolio and talk about my retirement plans. I told them, "Thanks, but I have already retired, am on a cross country bicycle ride, and at this moment am standing on the Continental Divide." The call was short. So, don't think you have to find an expert or do everything a for-profit consultant might say. You can likely do this on your own with a little planning and discipline. In fact, my advisor, who is older than I am, told me the he wished he could have retired as early as I did.

Helpful Exercises

Here are some questions to help you look more closely at your savings and investment amounts and plans.

Add up all your emergency fund money. This would be savings accounts or CDs. You can include funds in your checking that are greater than one month's budget.

Emergency Fund Amount: _____

Consider your situation and decide on a target emergency fund to have on hand. Enter this below.

Emergency Fund Target Amount: _____

If your emergency fund is already greater than the target, nice job! Consider moving the excess into investments. If your saved amount is less, add a savings category to your budget and set an amount to save monthly.

Monthly Savings toward an Emergency Fund:

_____

Add up all your current investments. These could be stocks, bonds, 401(k), 403(b), IRAs, rental property, etc.

Investment Amount Total: _____

If your emergency fund is taken care of, consider how much a month you would like to budget toward investment savings. Perhaps you can increase your amount if you are already investing. Or, if you have room in your budget, consider saving for the emergency fund and investing at the same time.

Monthly Savings into Investments:

_____

CHAPTER 5 - LOANS AND DEBT

It would be nice if loans and debt could be avoided entirely, but the reality in our world today is that this would be extremely difficult to impossible for most people. There are many opinions on loans and debt. Many ideas exist about whether we should borrow and if we should take on debt or not. Thomas Jefferson once said, "Never spend your money before you have it." King Solomon in Proverbs 22 states, "The rich rule over the poor, and the borrower is slave to the lender." With so many opinions, let's try to determine some reasonable guidelines for good financial choices.

When To Borrow

One of the most commonly asked questions seems to be when a person should borrow. My personal philosophy is to only borrow for large purchases, such as a house or a car. Everything else should be budgeted or saved for. Of course, many factors come into play. If interest rates are very high, then we may need to delay a large purchase, or perhaps save money for a less expensive used vehicle. If we already have a couple of loans, then it is probably best to put off another purchase that would result in additional debt.

As you get more established, and your savings and investments grow, it is quite possible to save money for a replacement vehicle and not take out any kind of loan. This has been true in my life as I have gotten older, and paired with my philosophy to only purchase pre-owned vehicles, it is even more attainable.

I have been asked, "How can I prepare for taking on debt?" I think this question shows great maturity in approaching borrowing. We can prepare in advance to make handling the debt more successful. For instance, one preparation is saving up a higher down payment amount. Often, home loans will offer a better interest rate if the down payment is higher. This is because there will be less risk to the lender. In addition, if a down payment is 20% or more, then a buyer will not have to pay the private mortgage insurance (PMI) premium, which is in addition to the interest and principal portions of a payment. Another way that we can prepare for more debt is to look at our monthly budget and start making changes ahead of time. We will need to be able to make our loan payment each month, so we may need to reduce some expenses or discretionary spending in order to make room for the new loan payment. How you maneuver this is up to you, based on your priorities in the budget. Finally, since many loans will require a down payment, we can start early to save the down payment amount well before we make the purchase. This savings amount would also need to be worked into our monthly budget.

How Much House Can I Afford?

When shopping for a home, you may be told by realtors and lenders how much house you can afford. Be wary of that kind of advice. Those in the industry are typically making money from a commission. It may be in their best interest to get you to spend as much as possible on a home, resulting in higher commissions into their pockets. I would encourage you to look out for your own best interest and think carefully about how much debt you want to take on. This payment may be something that you will have to deal with for 30 years. One number I see recommended is that your house payment and related amounts should not be more than 28% of your gross income. I would say that percentage should be the absolute maximum, but it would be much better to stay well below that percentage.

For example, a $50,000 household income would result in a 28% monthly amount of $1,167 (= $50,000 * 0.28 / 12) toward a house loan. At about a 5% interest rate, realtors and lenders might tell you that you can afford a home price up to about $180,000. I like to tell people to look for a home price at around two or two and a half times your annual income, or more in the range of $100,000 to $125,000. This will give you much more freedom to save and not stretch or stress your monthly budget. Remember that a home loan is a long-term commitment.

Down Payments

Regarding down payments, most loans require a certain amount for a down payment. For vehicles, this amount may vary. Some new car loans may be offered with no money down, but for used cars, which I strongly encourage everyone to consider, a down payment will almost always be required if you borrow. Check with your local bank or lender, because they may offer better rates than a dealer. For home loans, down payments vary by loan type. Some down payments are as low as 3%, but a larger down payment may well be to your advantage. If it is possible to put 20% down on a home loan, you can avoid the PMI premium from the beginning. If not, once your loan to value (LTV or the amount you owe divided by the home value) is below 80%, you can pay for an appraisal and get the PMI amount removed from your payment.

Existing Debt

It may be that you have some existing debt you would like to eliminate. This debt could be credit card debt, a car loan, a home mortgage, student loans, personal loans, and so forth. You would need to decide which debt to attack first. In general, I recommend initially paying off the highest interest rate debt. The debt with the highest interest rate, normally credit card debt, will be the debt that costs the most in interest. Some argue to pay off the loan with the smallest balance first, and that strategy does have some mental or psychological benefit of eliminating one full loan. But financially, the best strategy is to pay off the loan with the highest interest rate first.

There is not an easy or magic solution to eliminating debt. It is simply a matter of paying as much extra against a loan that you can possibly afford. If you have a credit card debt with a 15% to 20% interest rate, it may be best to even suspend savings temporarily to eliminate debt with such a high cost in interest. It can help to cut out ALL discretionary spending. You may need to look at selling unused or unneeded items through services like eBay or Craigslist in order to free up funds to apply toward a debt. And any reduction in monthly spending would allow that extra money to be paid toward eliminating a debt. I will discuss details on how to reduce spending in a later chapter. You may have to be ruthless about not eating out, dropping memberships you don't need, and eliminating other spending to apply extra money to a debt. It may not be easy, but it can be done. The idea is to sacrifice for a short period of time in order to have a better financial situation and security in the long-term.

Another question that comes up is related to the choices of paying a debt off early or saving more. For high interest loans, I would recommend paying off those debts as soon as you can. For lower interest loans, maybe at 6 or 7% or less, the choice is less clear. Money saved long-term in the stock market could average 7% or so, but this does require self-discipline to save those funds and not spend them on something else. But like I mentioned previously, there is the mental aspect of having less debt and not needing to make a loan payment. Once a loan is paid off, then you essentially will receive a raise. You will have the payment amount free to do other things with each month once a loan is retired. Essentially, high-interest loans are better to be paid off early, but the choice between saving and using that amount for a lower interest debt is more of a personal priority choice.

This idea of paying off debt soon or at least earlier than the normal loan length was something that I learned in my younger years that has stuck with me. My good friend Bob and I were discussing home loans and mortgages. I was still in high school and had never taken out any kind of a loan at that point in my life. Bob showed me a loan amortization table that detailed the interest and principal amounts of each payment. He explained that so little was going toward the loan principal in those early years that extra payments early on would have huge impact on how soon a loan could be paid off. An amortization table is a table or schedule that lists each monthly payment expected on the loan, and the table often includes the amount of interest and principal in each loan payment. Interest is the fee or cost of borrowing money, and the principal is the original amount borrowed.

For example, consider a $100,000 loan at a 5% annual interest rate for 30 years. Listed in the next table is part of the amortization table showing the first 4 payments and the last 4 payments. The payment each month is the same amount of $536.82. But early in the loan, most of each payment is interest. As we pay more and more of the balance on the loan, less interest is needed from each payment. If I make an extra principal payment of around $121 early in the life of the loan, then I would eliminate an entire payment at the end of the loan. It would be paid off one month early since the extra principal would essentially "jump" me down one line or month in the amortization table since the loan balance would be reduced by a monthly principal amount.

If I wait until close to the end of my 30-year mortgage to make an extra principal payment, then it would require an extra principal payment of over $500 to reduce my loan length by one month. Paying extra on a loan makes much more of an impact if we can pay extra principal early in the life of the loan. You can make the extra payment small and do it monthly, or you can make a large extra payment at the end of each year if you had extra cash available. But any extra principal paid against the loan will be very helpful and result in shortening the length of the loan and save money by paying less interest. Paying extra each monthly will save slightly more interest than paying the same lump sum at the end of the year.

Payment #	Principal	Interest	Payment	Loan Balance
1	$120.15	$416.67	$536.82	$99,879.85
2	$120.65	$416.17	$536.82	$99,759.20
3	$121.16	$415.66	$536.82	$99,638.04
4	$121.66	$415.16	$536.82	$99,516.38
...	...	...	...	...
357	$527.96	$8.86	$536.82	$1,598.44
358	$530.16	$6.66	$536.82	$1,068.28
359	$532.37	$4.45	$536.82	$535.91
360	$535.91	$2.23	$538.14	$0.00

When To Be Debt Free

Another question that has come up in my conversations is that of when to be debt free. This is a long-term goal and one plan will not work for everyone. If you enter the work force early, then you may be able to be debt free much sooner than someone who entered the work force later, perhaps due to additional years in school. It is a worthy financial goal, and certainly I wanted to be debt free well before I retired. Some do enter retirement and still have a home mortgage, but I did not want to have any debt when I reached retirement.

In my case, I no longer took out any vehicle or auto loans after I was about 39 years old. I could have avoided auto loans before that, but I had purchased a new vehicle and took advantage of a 0% interest offer. My current strategy of always buying used vehicles will allow me to avoid auto loans in the future. My wife and I had eliminated home mortgage debt by the time we were around 40 years old. I think a goal of eliminating all debt, loans, mortgages, etc. by the time you have been in the workforce for 20 years is a very realistic goal if you budget and exercise financial discipline. You may very well be able to be debt free before even working 20 years.

Eliminating debt will require discipline to make extra payments and avoid the temptation to buy new things that are wants rather than needs. It does require some work to stay motivated and stick to the task of eliminating debt. I would encourage you to track progress on these goals to be able to see those balances falling and getting smaller. Look further down the road and consider the additional freedom and flexibility that you will have once one or more debts are eliminated. I personally had to realize that eliminating debt was in my long-term best interest while accumulating debt to buy some of the toys and new, expensive vehicles that people around me were buying was not in my long term financial best interest.

Helpful Exercises

Use the form shown in the next table to get a better grasp of your current debts and loans. This will allow you to see what loan you may want to try to pay off first. There are columns for principal and interest, which may not be available from your lender. These are easily calculated, but you will need to know the interest rate, the loan balance, and the payment amount. I will provide some examples.

Interest Amount = (Balance * Annual Interest Rate) / 12

Note that interest rate should be a decimal number, not a percentage: 5% = 0.05

From the above amortization table example, we have a $100,000 loan balance with a 5% interest rate, so:

Interest Amount = ($100,000 * 0.05) / 12 = $416.67

Once we have the interest amount, we can find the principal amount for a payment.

Principal Amount = Payment Amount − Interest Amount

For the same example:

Principal Amount = $536.82 - $416.67 = $120.15

Let's do an example for a credit card balance. Assume a $3,000 credit card balance at 17.5% with a minimum payment of $60 per month.

Interest Amount = ($3,000 *0.175) / 12 = $43.75

Principal Amount = $60 - $43.75 = $16.25

Loan	Balance	Payment Amount	Payment Interest	Payment Principal
Sample House	$100,000	$536.82	$416.67	$120.15
Sample Credit Card	$3,000	$60.00	$43.75	$16.25

CHAPTER 6 - CREDIT CARDS

Credit cards... for many it is a love / hate relationship. It seems like you almost must have at least one credit card to function today, but they can also allow you to get into trouble. Let's take a close look at credit cards to see if they are a tool or a curse.

A credit card *can be* a financial tool that allows you to purchase items on credit. You open a credit card account with one of many financial firms, and you can make purchases using the card and then pay the card issuer later. If the balance you have accumulated on the card is paid off on time each month when the statement is issued, then you will not have to pay interest. On the other hand, if you are unable to pay the amount owed in full or pay it late, then you will be charged interest and possibly late fees.

Before the rise of debit cards, a credit card was usually required to make any kind of online purchase, reserve a rental car, reserve a hotel, and transact business over the phone. Now that debit cards are very common, they can be used in most every case in place of a credit card. This reduces the need to have a credit card in today's economy.

Advantages

Credit cards are not all gloom and doom. If you are diligent about paying off your balance and not get behind, then there are some advantages. For one thing, a credit card can help you build your credit rating. By having this credit account and paying it on time, you can build a positive credit history. It is important to not carry a balance, and certainly to not make a late payment. Another advantage is that many credit cards offer some kind of rewards program. You can earn miles for travel, points for gift cards, cash back, and other perks based on how much you spend each month. But again, discipline is key. If you carry a balance and must pay interest, the benefit of any rewards may be completely negated. Credit cards can often be more convenient than carrying a lot of cash. A lost card is easier to deal with than losing a large amount of cash. Additionally, credit cards are often taken by businesses that may not take a personal check, making them convenient and a commonly accepted form of payment.

Disadvantages

One of the biggest disadvantages is that a credit card offers a big temptation of easy money. They provide the opportunity to make purchases, often large purchases, that a person may not be able to afford to pay off quickly. If this happens for several months in a row, a large balance at a high interest rate could put the card holder into a large debt quickly. Furthermore, getting behind on payments will lead to late fees and hurt your credit score.

According to creditcards.com the average interest rate on a credit card is over 16%.[5] To put this in perspective, if you carried a balance from month to month of $2,000, you would have to pay $28 each month or $340 a year to just cover the interest.

From TransUnion.com, the average balance or debt per credit card holder is $5,465.[6] Using this average balance figure, a credit card user would pay $77 per month in interest or $929 each year just to cover the accrued interest on that balance. In addition, some credit cards require annual fees to maintain the account. This often is the case with high reward program cards. There are numerous credit cards available with no annual fee, so this disadvantage is easy to avoid.

Credit cards can then have these disadvantages: temptation of easy money, high interest rates, credit rating risk, and annual fees. Considering the disadvantages, I normally do not recommend credit cards for those in college or that do not yet have full time employment. I believe it is better to be established with a steady income, using a budget, and tracking your spending carefully before attempting to introduce a credit card into the mix. In most cases a debit card can fill the need that used to require a credit card. And a debit card will generally not let you overspend your account balance, since it does not offer credit.

Getting Out Of Trouble

Let's say that someone has built up a large debt using credit cards. How might they be able to get out of that situation? First, it is very important to destroy any credit cards and close out all credit card accounts. This will tend to "stop the bleeding" or prevent additional charges from increasing the debt amount further. Next, it will be necessary to pay much more than the minimum payment due in order to start paying more than interest and reduce the total balance on the card.

If more than one card has a balance, it is imperative to pay at least the minimum and not miss any payments on any of the credit card accounts. Missing payments will result in late and possibly penalty fees, which will only exacerbate the issue. If there is more than one card with a balance, it then becomes a choice of which one to try to pay off first. The best financial option would be to pay off the card with the highest interest rate first. This will save the most in interest on the overall balance. If most of the cards have a similar interest rate, then I would pay off the card with the smallest balance first, and then roll that extra payment amount into the payment on the credit card with the next highest balance. This will be a psychological boost as fewer cards will have a debt to be paid.

Another option if you have multiple credit cards with a balance is to take out a consolidation loan. This loan from a bank or credit union will consolidate all your credit card debt into one loan with one payment. All the credit card balances will be paid off by the consolidation loan, and you should take this opportunity to close out all credit cards to prevent further use. Some lenders may require this as part of the consolidation loan process. Ideally, you will be able to obtain a loan with a lower interest rate than the credit cards.

As with any financial goal, paying off credit card debt should be budgeted into your monthly expense budget. Create another budget category and budget the amount needed or available to pay off your credit card debt as quickly as possible. It will often be necessary and certainly helpful to cut spending as much as you can in order to more quickly eliminate the high interest credit card debt. It may take some time and discipline, but your financial health depends on it.

Helpful Exercises

Use the following table to create a list of all your credit cards, along with their balances, interest rates, and minimum payments. You can also enter your desired payment for budgeting purposes.

Credit Card	Annual Interest Rate	Balance	Minimum Payment	Desired Payment
TOTALS				

CHAPTER 7 - LARGE PURCHASES

One area of spending that I would like to cover in more detail is that of large purchases or big-ticket items. These can vary by situation or person, but in general, I consider these types of items to be purchases like a vehicle, house or property, and in some cases furniture or expensive electronics. It is possible to get into trouble with these items if caution is not exercised. But in addition, large purchases can offer opportunities for saving money and reducing expenses if approached carefully.

I am sure the idea is not new, but I recommend some sort of waiting period before making large purchases. And the larger the cost, the longer the waiting period should be. Time periods are not fixed, and you should adopt this approach using waiting times that work best for you. For instance, for a large item such as furniture, appliances, or electronics, I like to wait at least a week before purchasing. In other words, if I decide I want a new dishwasher, I will use at least a week of time to review options, research reliability, and consider alternatives before making the purchase. For a vehicle, new or used, a month is a good amount of time to weigh your options and search for good buys before spending such a large amount of money. For something very expensive like a house or property, I may wait three months from when I first think I want to buy that item. These waiting periods have often given me enough of a pause that I ended up spending less money or found a less expensive option that might not have been obvious in those first few days of emotional window shopping.

Vehicles

A new or used vehicle may be one of the first major purchases that a newly married couple or a single person with a new job will make. Often, when we finish college or trade school and find ourselves with a much larger income than we used to have, our minds wander to thoughts of buying a new or better vehicle. My first word of advice is to not even go to test drive a vehicle unless you have decided that buying one is necessary. The test drive often is the edge of a slippery slope toward more debt.

So, what kinds of questions might we ask ourselves before walking onto that new or used vehicle lot? First, do I really need it? If my current vehicle is working, then perhaps I could get it detailed or cleaned and waxed to make it look its best. Maybe I just need to fix a few minor issues to be satisfied with my current vehicle for a while longer. If on the other hand my trusty Ford just broke its crankshaft, as happened to me early in married life, then perhaps a replacement vehicle is more of a need than a want at that point.

For married couples, it might be possible to share one car. My wife and I have done this on several occasions during different seasons of life. If work schedules permit, then one person may be able to drop off the other person at work. It does require another trip to pick up the carless person after work, but it allows a large amount of expenses to be avoided if only one shared vehicle could be utilized. A small increase in gas cost might happen, but savings from repairs, maintenance, tags, fees, insurance, interest, and other areas add up quickly. This option might be seriously considered if a large debt is still owed on one of the vehicles.

Another option to help if one car is shared is that of biking to work. I have biked to work at different times during my working years. Sometimes showers are available at work, which allow you to get a workout and some exercise while biking to work, and still being able to clean up before the workday begins. I have even owned a couple of electric bikes and used them for getting to work or doing errands around town. In both cases, the electric bike was less than $1,000 and provided hundreds of gas and repair-free miles. Many electric bikes have a range of 15 to 20 miles on a full battery charge, and since you do not have to push hard to pedal, it is likely that you would never break a sweat.

If it turns out that a vehicle purchase is indeed necessary, it is helpful to be aware of all the up-front costs associated with a new vehicle. The purchase price is only part of the story. Many states require the payment of sales and excise tax on vehicle purchases. Tag and other fees along with registration may also be required in your state. In addition, vehicle insurance will need to be paid. For a replacement vehicle, the insurance cost may not change, but if you are adding a vehicle, the insurance cost will be an additional recurring expense.

There can also be a large difference in the total cost of a vehicle depending on whether it is new or used. Since sales and excise tax are based on the sales price, a less expensive used vehicle will result in a lower tax bill. Since a pre-owned vehicle will require a smaller loan, the loan can be paid off sooner and less interest will have to be paid. A new vehicle will depreciate, or lose value in the first few years, much more so than a used vehicle. Many times, a new vehicle will lose half of its value after three years.

Let's look at a basic example of purchasing a new versus a used vehicle. We will consider the effects of depreciation and the time value of money.

<u>Scenario 1</u> – Purchasing a new vehicle every three years over a six-year period.

We will assume a $40,000 new vehicle cost, and that it will

depreciate to be worth $20,000 in three years. In year 1, we spend $40,000 on the new vehicle. At the end of year 3, we trade-in the vehicle, now worth $20,000 and purchase another new vehicle for $40,000. At the end of year 6, the vehicle is worth $20,000 and can be traded or sold for that amount. Over the 6 years, we spent $40,000 total on vehicles. Our yearly cost was $40,000 / 6 or $6,667 per year.

Scenario 2 – Purchase a used vehicle and keep it for six years.

We will purchase a 3-year-old vehicle for $20,000 and keep it for the full six years. We will also save money on taxes and registration by not getting another vehicle after three years. At the end of year 6, our vehicle is now worth about $10,000 and can be sold or traded for that amount. Over the 6 years, we spent $10,000 on vehicles. Our yearly cost was $10,000 / 6 or $1,667 per year – or $5,000 less per year than buying new. Not only that, but had we taken the $20,000 extra we did not need for a new vehicle and invest it to earn an average return of just 4%, we would have an additional $25,306 in our account.

In other words, with this example, buying new would leave us with $0 of our original $40,000, while buying used would leave us with $35,306 left of our original $40,000!

Even if we choose to buy a new vehicle, there are actions that can be taken in order to save money in the long term. When I am considering a vehicle purchase, I spend a lot of time researching makes and models and their reliability. If I can shop carefully and purchase a model with high reliability, then my repair expenses over the life of that vehicle should be considerably lower. This may be less of an issue with a new vehicle, but it will be helpful for used vehicles or new vehicles that are kept beyond their basic warranty time limit. Consumer Reports reliability surveys are my primary source, but there are other ways to research reliability.

Another way to reduce recurring expenses is to shop for a vehicle with a higher fuel economy or higher miles per gallon (mpg) rating. The difference may be small, but over the life of a vehicle, better fuel economy will reduce our cost of fuel and be easier on our budget. You can use your average number of miles driven in a year to estimate your savings. For example, if we assume we will drive 20,000 miles per year, then we can do some calculations:

Vehicle with 20 mpg: 20,000 / 20 = 1,000 gallons of fuel per year

Vehicle with 40 mpg: 20,000 / 40 = 500 gallons of fuel per year

This difference of 500 gallons will be a savings of 500 * $2.57 = $1,285 per year at today's national average gas price. You can use your current or local gas price to do the same calculations. Over a ten- or twenty-year span, this savings can add up to something significant.

Another possible area of savings for a vehicle purchase is related to financing or taking out a loan. A dealer may not offer the best interest rate for a car purchase. Check with your local banks or credit unions to see what kind of rates are available on new or used cars. In many cases, a larger down payment could lower your interest rate, so this would be an option to consider. The bank or lender can calculate the total interest paid for different loans, and this information is helpful. Since interest is money that is lost and cannot be recovered, it is important to try to lower the amount borrowed and the length of the loan in order to lower the total interest paid over the life of the loan.

For instance, using some current interest rates and loan lengths:

A $40,000 new vehicle at 4.77% for 60 months results in

$5,038 in interest paid.

A $20,000 used vehicle at 5.26% for 36 months results in $1,663 in interest paid.

Similar calculations can be done with numerous online loan calculators, but the results show that in general, a lower length loan and a lower amount borrowed result in much less interest being paid.

Insurance

Another significant recurring cost related to vehicles is insurance. Depending on who you talk to, you will receive all kinds of advice related to vehicle insurance. I personally try to keep my insurance premiums low, but I must be careful that I have proper coverage. Many states have required minimum amounts, so those will have to be considered. The three main types of insurance that I consider when comparing options are liability, comprehensive, and collision. Liability coverage will pay someone else if I am at fault and damage their property or cause injury, but liability coverage will not pay for my vehicle if I am at fault. Comprehensive coverage pays for my vehicle damage due to causes other than a collision, such as theft, vandalism, fire, natural disasters or weather, and so forth. Collision coverage will pay for my vehicle if damaged in a collision that is my fault, or if I hit something, or if someone hits me but does not have insurance.

If you take out a loan to buy a vehicle, the lender will likely have requirements for minimum insurance, including liability, comprehensive, and collision coverage. The lender wants to be sure that they can be paid if the vehicle is damaged or a total loss while you still owe on the loan. You may not have a lot of choices to reduce your insurance cost in this situation, other than shopping different insurance companies.

If your vehicle is older, and the value is low, then it may be worth considering having only liability coverage. You would be responsible for fixing or replacing the vehicle if you have an accident, but your savings in lower premiums would help offset this cost. For me, if a vehicle is over ten years old, then I usually will only carry liability coverage. I know that my emergency fund or other savings can be utilized to replace a vehicle if necessary.

For a newer vehicle that still has a sizable value, comprehensive and collision coverage may still be desired. However, you can still look at different deductibles to save some money on premiums. The deductible amount is the amount that you would have to pay in the event of an accident. If my deductible is $1,000, and I have an accident and the damage is $4,000 to my vehicle, the insurance company would pay $3,000 and I would be responsible for the other $1,000 (my deductible amount). You do have to consider that for higher deductibles you would need to have that amount available in an emergency fund or savings. If I can choose a higher deductible, with a lower cost or premium, then I can calculate how many years it would take to save the difference in deductible costs (break even) if I had an accident and had to pay the higher deductible.

Deductible examples for our Hyundai Santa Fe:

Comprehensive and Collision Deductible Amount	Annual Premium	Premium Savings vs $500 Deductible per Year	Years to Break Even
$500	$653	-	-
$1,000	$507	$146	3.4
$2,500	$320	$333	6.0

You will need to make your own decision based on your situation. In my case, I never carry below $1,000 deductible on vehicles. As the vehicle ages I will raise the deductible to lower my premiums. Usually I will move my deductibles to $2,500 after the vehicle is 5 or 6 years old. Be sure that you can pay the deductible in the event of an accident, otherwise this can cause other problems if the vehicle cannot be repaired in a timely manner. In some minor cases, replacing a fender or bumper cover, the work can be done yourself if you have basic mechanical skills. Finally, shop insurance companies because rates can vary between different companies for the same coverage.

Vehicle Extended Warranties

My philosophy on extended warranties of any kind is to avoid them. This applies to vehicles as well. Repairs can be expensive at times, but I can improve my chances of not spending as much money on repairs by researching and purchasing vehicles with good reliability. Many times, vehicle extended warranties will have restrictions and fine print that may not pay for some types of repairs. I now buy only used vehicles to save money in the long term, but I usually buy a used vehicle with some portion of the factory power train warranty remaining. Most manufacturers will transfer that warranty to second owners, so I am able to drive the vehicle for a few years before I lose the original warranty.

If you choose to decline an extended warranty, be prepared to deal with some pressure from the sales or finance person at a dealership. They make money from selling the extended warranty, so they are often anxious to apply some pressure. As I think back over the last 6 to 8 vehicles that I have owned, none of them had any issues that would have been taken care of by an extended warranty. Since these warranties can cost from $1,500 to $2,500, I have saved around $15,000 or more by not buying vehicle extended warranties. That amount of money would have easily covered a major repair or two, had they happened. Buy smart and skip the extended warranty trap.

Let's recap. Over 6 years we can save a considerable amount of money by buying a used vehicle. We save more by having a car with better gas mileage. We save money by paying less interest where possible or even no interest if we pay cash. We save money on lower sales or excise taxes due to a lower purchase price. We can save money by buying a reliable vehicle and not buying an extended warranty. If that total savings were invested at 4%, then we end up with a sizable bonus in our investment account. The exact numbers on each of these items vary, but I think you can understand my philosophy and reasons for opting to purchase used vehicles instead of new ones.

Houses

The largest purchase most people will make is that of a home. There are numerous things to consider when purchasing a home, as many factors will affect the purchase price and cost of ownership. One of the most common aspects people think of is size. I would encourage you to consider carefully how large of a house is needed versus wanted. The size in square footage of a home will impact taxes, insurance, utilities, purchase price, the cost of furnishings, maintenance, cleaning cost or time, and many other issues that have a financial impact.

According to the American Enterprise Institute, the average house size has increased by more than 1,000 square feet from 1973 to 2015.[7] In 1973, the average house size of a new home was 1,600 square feet. By 2015, the new home size had ballooned to 2,687 square feet. In addition, the average household size (number of persons) has declined, resulting in nearly twice as many square feet per person in 2015 as compared to 1973. The cost of building a home, adjusted for inflation, has remained nearly constant at $116 per square foot. This means that in 1973, an average family had about $186,000 (in current dollars) tied up in a home. By 2015, the average family had nearly $312,000 tied up in a home. While property may appreciate or at least keep up with inflation, that extra $126,000 is not generating a return like other investments. Life is about choices, and most Americans are choosing to go bigger and larger.

Our family has not been immune to the lure of larger homes. The first home my wife and I purchased was about 1,300 square feet with three bedrooms. About 15 years later, we built a home with over 2,700 square feet of living space and an additional living space over the garage of 900 square feet! While we were living in this home, which we expected to retire in, we came to the realization that our money tied up in that house was not providing us much return on our investment. We made the conscious choice to downsize. We are now in an older three-bedroom home that is just over 1,600 square feet. We have three bedrooms, adequate living space, and much lower utilities, insurance, and taxes. We also were able to take a large amount of equity and invest it more wisely.

Taking our earlier example of ever-increasing house sizes, we can see the impact of choosing to live in a smaller space. If we assume the 1,600 square foot home costs about $186,000 and the 2,687 square foot home costs $312,000, then the difference in price alone is $126,000. This is ignoring savings on utilities, taxes, insurance, maintenance, and so forth. Over a 30-year time frame, if a person invests the $126,000 difference in stock index funds that return even 7%, then the future value of that amount is significant:

$126,000 * (1.07)^{30}$ = $126,000 * 7.612 = $959,112

Just choosing a smaller home could result in nearly an additional million dollars saved over a 30-year time frame! It really boils down to need versus want, so choose carefully. Do you want to live in a large house, or do you want the future option of retiring early, or travelling, or having more options in life, or giving more to charitable causes, etc.?

Beyond just the purchase price, financing and interest costs are a significant aspect of purchasing a home. Nearly all home loans will require a down payment, typically a percentage of the purchase price. Once again, a lower purchase price can be our friend. Many loans will require at least a 5% down payment, and buyers are required to also purchase PMI (Private Mortgage Insurance) if a down payment is less than 20%. In addition, interest rates may be lower with higher down payments. Here are some example down payments for a few purchase price amounts:

Sales Price	5% Down Payment	10% Down Payment	20% Down Payment
$125,000	$6,250	$12,500	$25,000
$200,000	$10,000	$20,000	$40,000
$300,000	$15,000	$30,000	$60,000

Now, if you do not put down 20% and must pay PMI as part of your mortgage payment, you can pay for another appraisal after you have built up at least 20% equity in the home. This would save the PMI amount for the remainder of the life of the loan even if you must pay it initially.

Regardless of the house price or loan amount or length, I would strongly encourage you to pay extra principal in order to pay the loan off early. This will result in less interest being paid over the life of the loan. My wife and I purchased our first home after we both graduated from college and began our first full time jobs. We knew that we wanted one of us to stay home with children after they were born, and we knew that we would need to be able to live on just one income at that point. So, we chose to put most of her take home pay towards the house. We made significant extra principal payments and were able to pay the home off early and save a large amount of interest.

The first time I became interested in finance was related to this very topic. It was related to a conversation with a friend (briefly mentioned in the last chapter). At the young age of 14, an older gentleman, Bob, explained the advantage of making extra principal payments on home loans. It was like an epiphany for me to realize that, by adding an extra $50 to my mortgage payment each month, I could greatly reduce the life of the loan and save thousands of dollars in interest. These early discussions prompted me to make better choices when I did begin to take on loans and debt. I am very thankful for such a fine friend as Bob.

One final word on home loans, I recommend that you shop around for lower loan interest rates and look carefully at fees. Different banks and lenders have different loan rates, and fees can vary greatly. I recall one loan where I did not ask enough questions and was surprised by an $800 "loan application fee" when we closed on the house. That was a tough lesson and I have not made that mistake again. It is very important to ask a bank or lender to detail each and every fee and cost that will be associated with a loan.

Home insurance costs can vary widely depending on the coverage. If your house is in a flood plain, then flood insurance may be required. If not required, but a rare flood event could still impact your home, it should be carefully considered anyway. The same decisions concerning deductibles are applicable for home insurance as with auto insurance. In some cases, the roof deductible may be higher or different than the standard deductible. Shop different companies and compare coverages very carefully. I typically carry a $2,500 or $5,000 deductible on my home, knowing that I can take care of minor issues and the insurance is meant to cover a large loss in the case of a significant event.

Here is a comparison of different deductibles on our approximately 1,650 square foot home:

Deductible Amount	Annual Premium	Cost Difference	Years to Break Even
$1,000	$1,365	-	-
$2,500	$1,042	$323	4.6
$5,000	$723	$642	6.2

So, you will need to consider how much you can pay (the deductible amount) in the event of a loss, and how often you think you may have to file a claim. In my experience the primary claims have been for a water leak resulting in interior flooding and for a damaged roof in a hailstorm. Your most probable claims may be different depending on where you live and your situation.

Helpful Exercises

Use the table below to fully understand your vehicle loan information. It can be used when considering a vehicle purchase.

Vehicle Price	Interest Rate	Loan Length	Payment Amount

Use the table below to evaluate your vehicle insurance coverage and premiums, or it can be used to compare different premiums and deductibles if you are shopping insurance.

Vehicle	Coverage	Deductible	Premium

Use the table below to evaluate different house prices, loan lengths, and payment amounts.

House Price	Interest Rate	Loan Length	Payment Amount

Use the table below to evaluate different home insurance rates and deductibles.

Company	Coverage	Deductible	Premium

CHAPTER 8 - ADVICE FOR COUPLES

If you are married, or planning to get married, then financial decisions may be more involved. In my case, my wife and I have similar financial habits, or they are at least similar enough that we have been able to work through minor disagreements. But disagreements are inevitable, and we can ideally resolve them with minimal conflict.

If You Are Single

If you are single, then the financial decisions may be solely yours to make. Some decisions impact others around us, but a single person will not have some of the interactions with a partner to work through. However, if you are single and planning to get married, or are already engaged, then there will be value to discussing financial topics with your future spouse.

Many of these topics have already been covered, but I will list some possible questions to work through and discuss if your single days are numbered.

What are each of your financial habits? In other words, are you a saver, a spender, or one who does not think or deal much with financial matters? Is your future spouse a saver or a spender?

What are each of your future financial goals and plans? Do you want to save for a large purchase? Do you want to retire early or at a certain age?

What are each of your expectations related to large purchases?

Do you want to purchase a house? Do you want to purchase a vehicle soon? These choices can have widely varying costs associated with them depending on the personal wants and desires of each individual.

What financial baggage, good or bad, is coming into the relationship? Do either of you have existing debts, including student loans? How will those be addressed? Assuming you each have one or more bank, savings, or investment accounts, will those be kept separate or merged?

Every detail will not have to be worked out immediately, but an honest discussion about financial habits, hopes, and dreams can help to prevent some future disagreements. Your decisions as a couple may be different from ours, and that is perfectly fine.

If You Are Married

If you are married and have not come to a common ground on many financial matters, then many of the above questions would be worth discussing as a married couple. Even if you agree on most topics, what are your future hopes and dreams?

In our case, our dreams have changed over time. We still need to come to a consensus or some common ground about what we want to do financially, but some of our goals in our early married years were different from our goals and plans in recent years. Some of the changes were due to our stage in life, but some were simply due to a change in philosophy.

Early on, we chose to build a large home and buy new vehicles, but about a decade later we had decided that downsizing to a smaller home and purchasing used vehicles was best for us financially. As we thought about our future in our 20s and mid-30s, we certainly did not plan to retire early, but by our late 30s we had started to consider the option of an early retirement.

My best advice is to communicate with each other. This is valuable for any topic, but especially for financial matters. Also, try not to have an immovable position. When I was younger, I was much less likely to compromise on issues we disagreed on, but I realize now that our life together and our relationship is more important than a certain purchase or financial choice. Age does bring more wisdom, and I am grateful for that.

CHAPTER 9 - CHILDREN AND FINANCES

Once we talk about couples and finances, the next logical step is talking about children and finances. There are several approaches that we can take in this discussion, but the main two questions I have heard are similar to the following.

How will having children impact my finances?

How can I teach or instruct my children about finances?

Added Expenses

Adding children to the picture will certainly influence your finances and budget. Early on, there will be the expense of diapers, formula, clothing, and so forth. As they get older, activities, food, and general care will need to be included in your budget. In the teenage years, the possible costs of a vehicle purchase and paying for college can become a concern. These expenses will vary from family to family, but it is important to be aware of and not be surprised by additional expenses related to children.

Regarding college expenses, my advice is to start saving early, soon after they are added to your family. College expenses continue to rise and starting to save early is a great way to save more by the time they graduate from high school. One method is to look at the average cost of attendance for a few possible college options, and then adjust that for inflation for the number of years until they attend. For instance, if we assume $20,000 per year, we will need $80,000 to cover four years. If we assume an average inflation rate of 3%, and 18 years until college starts, our adjusted cost for four years would be:

$$\$80{,}000 * (1.03)^{18} = \$80{,}000 * 1.7 = \$136{,}000$$

Perhaps we feel that our child might be able to cover half of that cost with scholarships, grants, work-study, and a job. This would leave $68,000 that we need to save. If we use a bond index fund that returns 4% annually, we can use a savings calculator to figure out the annual or monthly amount we need to set aside. Doing this indicates that we need to save about $217 per month, for 18 years. The later that we start saving, the more that we would need to save each month. Enter your own numbers and make your own calculations, but this is the basic process that I have used.

Also, many states offer a 529 college savings plan. This plan often has tax advantages that would make it beneficial to save using your state plan. This will vary by state, so investigate your own state's options. The plan information should show average return rates for the different fund options, if available.

Besides college, purchasing a vehicle for a child is another large, lump sum expense. Some families may not opt to do this, but other families want to purchase a vehicle when the child is able to drive, or when they leave for college or move out on their own. I am reminded of a story by a good friend some years back. He had a good income, so he chose to purchase a new truck for his oldest child when they were able to drive. This was all great until the second of his four children was old enough to drive. He had set the bar very high by purchasing a new vehicle for the oldest child, and now had to do the same for the other three. His advice after that experience was to be very careful about what vehicle was purchased for the first child of several children!

Some families ask the child to earn and save the money for a vehicle by working. Other families may match what the child has saved and pay half of the cost. Adding a vehicle or a young driver will increase auto insurance rates, so this will need to be accounted for in the budget. Adding a young male driver will increase rates more than adding a young female driver. These are all things to keep in mind and evidence that your budget will need to adjust and be modified from time to time.

Teaching Children

Just as important as budgeting for the expense of children is the responsibility of teaching our children about finances. If I want them to make good choices, then I must teach, model, and demonstrate good choices in my own life.

In our family, one of the earliest ways that we began educating our children was with an allowance. This could be given weekly or monthly, and I believe the actual amount is less important than the opportunity to help them learn. The allowance was not a gift but was given with the idea that they had some responsibilities. Small tasks or chores around the house were expected of them. The amount increased as they got older, but having some amount of money allowed them to choose how to spend it. Helping them make these spending choices were teaching moments in themselves.

Since our family tithes, or gives to our church, we modelled and taught this to our children. We would usually give the allowance in smaller bills or with some change, so that they could easily figure out what 10% would be and give that amount from their allowance. I know that in my own life, learning to do this early and forming a habit made it much easier as my income increased from my teenage and into my young adult years.

If one of our children wanted to purchase something that was a sizable cost for them, such as a guitar, we would often pay half of this big expense, and they would pay the other half. Or rather than just purchase an expensive gift that was more than we might normally do for a birthday or Christmas, we would offer to pay half and let them pay the other half. This helped them buy something that was more costly and might be difficult to buy on their own. But it also allowed them to have some involvement and it did cost them something. They were often more responsible and careful with an item that they had to help purchase with their own funds because they felt ownership.

Another way that we have tried to teach our children about finances is to talk about our family's financial choices and the reasons behind them. This was more meaningful as our children got older. If we are purchasing a car, we might talk about why we purchased that vehicle. We can explain how it meets our family's needs and why we purchased a used vehicle versus a new one. We might not get into the specifics of price and cost, but if we are not buying the kind of vehicle they see other families purchasing, then this can be a learning experience.

As we downsized our house and reduced possessions a few years back, this was a teaching moment for our children. We used this time to explain why we felt that these were the right choices for us. They had questions about why we were selling our large home and moving into a smaller and much less expensive home. They had questions about why we were selling or donating many things that we had accumulated. Although the children could see the choices that we were making and the actions that we were taking, it was important to talk about those choices and explain the reasons behind them. We did not take advantage of every opportunity to teach them on financial matters, but we did try to talk about finances and our choices on many occasions. I would encourage you to take advantage of those opportunities to have age-appropriate financial discussions with your children.

Helpful Exercises

Estimate the cost of college for each of your children, record how much you have saved so far for college, record how many years until they start college, then calculate how much you need to save each month to reach your savings goal, whatever that may be. Online resources can be helpful to determine the average cost of a public college or university. A simple method would be to multiply the annual cost of college by four (to cover a total of four years) and then divide that total by the number of years until your child will begin college. This is simplified and does not account for inflation or earned interest, but it will be a start. For example, if my child is 6 years old, then they will likely start college in 12 years. If the cost of college is $20,000 per year, then a total for four years would be $80,000. Taking $80,000 and dividing by 12 results in a yearly amount of $6,667 per year that would need to be saved. The monthly amount to save would be $555 per month.

Child	Age	Years to College	Estimated Cost	Amount Saved	Amount Needed	Savings per Month

CHAPTER 10 - RETIREMENT

In a sense, many of our financial choices are made with a future goal in mind. This has certainly been true with me as it relates to the goal of retirement. Many of the reasons that our family has lived more frugally and not gone into sizable debt has to do with living with less now in order to have more options later. I read of financial experts recommending that you should not have debt or a mortgage by the time you reach retirement. And I think, "Of course you shouldn't!" We have more than enough years while working that we should be able to eliminate debt before retirement. And if we still have outstanding debt, that may be a good reason to delay retirement.

So, when is the right, proper or best time to retire? Well, the answer will vary vastly from person to person. I personally remember sitting through at least three funerals near the time I turned 40. In every case, the person worked up until at least their social security retirement age, perhaps 65 or 67. But within a year, there was a health issue or some other unexpected situation that resulted in their death. They all had plans of doing things with friends or family during retirement, but it turned out that they did not have the time. This was a sobering experience for me and a turning point in my desire to retire earlier than 'normal'.

I believe that there are several factors to consider related to retirement timing. These include purpose, timing, and extent. What will be your purpose during retirement, or after full time employment ends? Some want to spend time with family or grandkids; some may want to take up new interests or devote more time to hobbies; some may want to serve others and give back to their community; and others may want to travel. Or, it could be a mix of these ideas and many more. In any case, according to a study published in the PLOS Medicine journal, moderate physical activity can extend life expectancy.[8] One of my personal goals during retirement was to stay active and not be dormant.

Each person will also have to consider the timing of their retirement. There could be many reasons to choose a certain time to retire, and each situation is unique. Some may want to work until the Social Security retirement age. Some may very much enjoy their work and continue to work beyond a typical retirement age. Others may have a retirement plan at work that requires a certain number of years of service to draw full benefits. Still others may want to retire early. In my case, I did not have a retirement plan, but I did save and invest aggressively over my working years. This has allowed me to retire early, before I was 45, but your choice of the best time to retire is your own. If someone decides to retire early, they will need to be relatively sure that savings and other income generating investments will be able to cover expenses. Even with early retirement, Social Security is often available which can give slight boost to income once that specific age is reached.

Finally, there is the additional option of full versus partial retirement. If savings and investments do not allow a full retirement, there could be the option of a partial retirement. A part time or side job could provide enough income, in addition to any savings, to bridge the years until full retirement is possible. Again, every situation is unique, and what worked for me and my family may not work for you.

How Much To Save

One of the most common questions I have heard is "How much should I save for retirement?"

It is not a question of how much to save, but rather a question of generating income to cover expenses in retirement. Generating or creating income could be done with dividends or returns from investments, part time work, rental property, or other sources. The amount of income needed in retirement is directly related to the budget of expenses. The lower your budget of expenses, the less you would need to have saved or the less income you would need to earn or generate. For this reason, I believe that it is extremely important to have all debt paid off before retirement and to lower expenses as much as reasonably possible, especially recurring expenses.

Trying to estimate living expenses during retirement can be challenging. It is possible to use a current budget and then adjust and remove expenses to try to arrive at a reasonable estimate. Some 'experts' will say that you will need 70 or 80% of your pre-retirement budget, but that is a complete guess and could very well be inaccurate. In my case, I removed all expenses related to children, since they would all be out of the house soon after retirement. I adjusted auto insurance down to only the vehicles we would have in retirement. Likewise, food budgets and other categories could be adjusted or at least estimated for just my wife and me. Of course, once this number is estimated, we still need to adjust annually for inflation up to the actual retirement age. Nothing is certain when we work with finances, and it is somewhat of an inexact science. However, with some reasonable estimates and work, I believe a useful number for annual expenses can be estimated for most situations.

So, let's say for example that you have done your best to estimate annual expenses in retirement and your annual budget amount is $45,000. Now what? Well, we need to generate that amount each year, adjusted for inflation, if we plan to retire and be able to cover our expenses. If you are retiring before the Social Security age, then you would need to be able to cover that full amount with savings, investments, and other income. Once you reach the Social Security age, Social Security income will cover part of those annual expenses.

In addition to Social Security, you may have other sources of income in retirement such as part time work, rental income if you have rental property, and so forth. Some people may have another retirement or pension that may begin at an age different from the Social Security age. These supplemental income streams would reduce the amount of income that would need to be generated directly from savings and investments.

But, let's assume for now that we need to generate all $45,000 of our annual expenses from our savings or investments. A common rule of thumb for using savings and investments in retirement is the 4% rule. The 4% rule basically states that based on historical stock and bond market data, someone should be able to withdraw 4% of the balance of their investments each year and not exhaust their investments in their lifetime. It also allows for an adjustment each year due to inflation. If we withdraw $45,000 this year, then we can withdraw about $45,000 * 1.02 = $45,900 the next year. This 4% rule gives us a reasonable guideline to determine how much we need to save into our investments before we can retire. The 4% rule also assumes that the amount is invested in a mix of stocks and bonds, and in my case, I have both stock and bond index funds. This rule will not work if all your money is in a savings account or CDs with a low rate of return.

Back to our example of needing $45,000 annually in retirement. If we intend to generate this completely from our investments (mostly stocks and bonds), then our investment total would need to be:

$45,000 / 4\% = \$45,000 / 0.04 = \$1,125,000$

However, if we can generate $15,000 a year from rental income, social security, part time work, or other annual income, then we would only need $30,000 annually from our investment portfolio. In this case our investment total would need to be:

$30,000 / 4\% = \$30,000 / 0.04 = \$750,000$

Once we know the investment amount needed to fund retirement, we can make a plan to reach that goal. This will vary greatly depending on how many years until retirement and how much we have saved so far. Let's use the investment goal of $1,000,000 and our average conservative estimate of a 7% return from mostly stocks to illustrate a few scenarios. Also, let's assume a retirement age of 55. These numbers can be generated from a savings calculator or even a spreadsheet or calculator if you know a few financial formulas.

Current Age	Years Until 55	Monthly Savings	Total at 55
20	35	$555	$1,005,416
25	30	$815	$1,000,076
30	25	$1,230	$1,002,200
35	20	$1,910	$1,000,774
40	15	$3,140	$1,001,067
45	10	$5,750	$1,001,043

Please don't be discouraged by this chart. This is only one example. However, you can clearly see that starting to save early is extremely important. The longer we wait to save, the more we need to save to catch up. In some cases, it will not be possible to save enough to retire at a particular age. There are many aspects of this over which you have control. First, starting to save early, even a smaller amount, will be a significant advantage later in life. Also, you can adjust the retirement age to allow more years to save. If annual expenses in retirement can be reduced, then less savings is needed. Additionally, any amount of income that can be generated in retirement other than using savings and investments, will reduce the amount that needs to be saved. If you are wanting to retire before the Social Security age, then you would only need to cover all your annual expenses in retirement until that time. Once Social Security income begins, then the amount needed from investments will be reduced. This can be calculated as well, but it is more involved and will not be covered in detail here. You can start by visiting www.ssa.gov.

Helpful Exercises

Use the questions below to help define your retirement plans.

Current age _____

Expected retirement age _____

Years until retirement _____

Expected retirement expenses _____

Current retirement savings _____

Retirement savings needed to provide 4% annual withdrawals

_____

Monthly savings needed to reach retirement savings goal

_____

(A savings calculator can be found online to use current savings, years to retirement, total savings needed and then adjust monthly savings to find out what amount is needed to meet your goal.)

CHAPTER 11 - PRACTICAL SPENDING ADJUSTMENTS

Let's assume that you have set up a budget and are tracking your expenses. Let's also assume that you want to save for some large financial goals, like retirement, but there does not seem to be much room in your budget and expenses to do so. How do we proceed from here?

If we want to save more for financial goals, then we have two options. We either need to increase our income in order to have more money to save, or we need to decrease our expenses in order to spend less and save more. This chapter is all about the practical details of spending less. Many of these suggestions are some that our family personally implemented. These are broken down by category.

Housing

Housing and the related expenses are typically one of the largest budget categories, but it also can be a great opportunity to reduce our ongoing expenses. While this may be one of the more difficult areas in which to reduce expenses, it is possible.

Downsizing our house or reducing our housing costs can have a tremendous impact on reducing expenses and even freeing up equity. This was one of the pivotal moments in our financial life. Our home, larger than we needed, was paid for, and the decision to downsize jumpstarted our retirement savings more than we had imagined. Any change can be difficult, but in the end, we are confident it was the right decision for us. The sale of our home and subsequent downsizing freed up a large amount of equity that was put into our retirement savings. But downsizing had additional effects of reducing our property taxes, reducing our utilities, and reducing our insurance. All these reductions combined to lower our entire budgeted housing expense category.

Additional savings related to housing can sometimes be found by shopping your homeowner's insurance. You may find a lower price at another company. Deductible amounts and the associated premiums should be researched to determine if a higher deductible is worth the savings for your situation.

Other expenses that may be reduced include repair costs or minor home improvement projects by doing much of the work yourself. Online resources are helpful for many small home repair jobs and improvements. Heating and cooling costs may be reduced by using a programmable thermostat and raising the set point in the summer and lowering it in the winter. Having our house a little warmer in the summer and a little cooler in the winter reduced the amount of time the system was running. We have found that our body acclimates to a few degrees of change without much difference in our comfort level.

Vehicles And Transportation

Another significant budget expense category can be vehicles and transportation. Savings in these expense areas are related to owning multiple vehicles, since we did not live in a large city and commute.

For a period, our family moved to having just one vehicle. The single vehicle option is not as difficult to deal with as some might think. One spouse might drop the other off at work and then drive to their own job. If possible due to your location, you may be able to walk or bike to work and not need a second vehicle. Moving to just one vehicle lowers the amount of money tied up in automobiles, but it also offers reduced expenses in the areas of auto insurance, repairs, maintenance, tag, and so forth. This could also be done as a temporary measure for a limited number of years.

When purchasing a vehicle, buying used will often result in lower up-front costs and less money lost to vehicle depreciation. The lower purchase price also reduces sales or excise tax that must be paid based on the purchase price. My personal philosophy is to buy used vehicles, but regardless of a new or used purchase it is helpful to make a smart purchase. I always consider reliability information to select a used vehicle that is one of the most reliable models or brands. Also, when making a vehicle selection, some consideration to fuel economy can lower the fuel costs over the life of that vehicle. All this information is easily available online, although reliability might require a subscription to Consumer Reports. When purchasing, avoid impulse or uneducated purchases. Set a time period of perhaps 30 days as a minimum amount of time to research and look at what is available before making a purchase. This tip and others boil down to doing adequate research.

As with our home, we can shop insurance coverage and look at different deductibles to lower our vehicle related costs. At a certain vehicle age and value, dropping to only liability coverage will save money on insurance premiums. It is important to have the ability to cover a high deductible amount if that is the option we choose.

Finally, purchasing a reliable model allows us to confidently not even consider extended warranties. I do not buy them on vehicles (or any other item, for that matter). They might be helpful on a rare occasion, but over my lifetime the cost of all the warranties will greatly exceed any savings from them. In fact, I do not recall a single instance where buying an extended warranty on a vehicle or any other large purchase like home electronics or appliances would have saved me money on that item due to a repair. By declining all extended warranties, I have saved tens of thousands of dollars over the course of my life

Minor maintenance items can be done yourself on many vehicles to save money on those expenses. Simple tasks like changing my own oil, replacing wiper blades, replacing air filters, and checking my tire pressure are not difficult. Other items that I have taken care of myself to save on vehicle spending including replacing vehicle batteries, cleaning upholstery and carpets with a rental machine, replacing spark plugs, and washing and waxing.

Other options for reducing vehicle or transportation expenses include biking, taking public transportation, or carpooling. These options might allow you to have a single vehicle or even no vehicle at all. In some cases, public transportation or carpool options can save on fuel and wear and tear on a vehicle. Consider carpooling with a coworker if you have a significant commute. Bicycling is another good choice. I have bicycled to work with several different jobs, and an inexpensive electric bike can allow for errands and other short trips around town without a vehicle. At one location where we lived close to a grocery store, my wife and I would bicycle to the store and bring home grocery in saddle bags or panniers. Aside from financial benefits, bicycling is also great exercise and easy on the knees.

Other Large Purchases

Other large purchases, such as higher priced electronics, appliances, more expensive tools, and some outdoor items should be considered carefully in order to avoid unnecessary spending. When possible, I research reliability of models and brands. This is easier for appliances and larger electronics via Consumer Reports. If I can purchase only reliable brands and models, then I save money in the long run. Also, it allows me to easily turn down the extended warranties for these items.

As I consider different models of appliances or electronics, I generally go with a less complex model when possible. Fewer features and less complexity typically equal fewer problems and better reliability. Only buy what is truly needed as far as features are concerned and avoid models with unnecessary features. It can be easy to fall into the trap of wanting an item with every possible feature, but this may be more expensive both immediately and in the long term.

For some items that are used less frequently, I will often rent what I need. Large tools that are only needed occasionally can be rented locally and I save the initial purchase cost and any maintenance or repair costs. I have decided that it is not necessary for me to own every large tool and outdoor item that I may ever need. But if I check rental prices and see that it may be comparably inexpensive to purchase the item, then that information helps me to decide if purchasing makes more sense.

Miscellaneous Expense Reductions

There are many ways to reduce spending and expenses in miscellaneous areas, so I will cover a long list of items below.

We work hard to keep our food budget in check. Eating out will quickly cause our food bill to balloon out of control. We do eat out but keep the number of times that we do so to only once or twice per week. This does mean that when I worked an office job, I would often bring my lunch from home. We will eat leftovers and refrain from throwing food away when possible. It is often easier to eat healthy at home than in a restaurant, so that gives us another reason to eat at home. The average American eats out four or five times a week, spending $232 per person per month on restaurant meals.[9] This works out to nearly $13.00 per meal eaten out. For us, we can prepare meals at home and eat for under $3 per meal per person.

Entertainment is a discretionary expense, but it can grow and become a significant expense. We started being more cautious and dropped cable TV years ago, and since then cord cutting has become the new normal. However, streaming services can stack up and quickly get as expensive. We only pay for one streaming service. We do not pay for cable or satellite television, and we manage just fine. Over the air television is still available, for the rare times that we need to watch a live sporting event or broadcast news.

Our cell phone bill was over $140 per month when we began to downsize. Thankfully, there are many more competitive options now to allow you to reduce your mobile phone bill. New options like Google Fi, Republic Wireless, and others offer monthly rates that are much less than they used to be. Our provider allows us to keep a low or even no data plan. I personally do not have data on my smartphone, utilizing Wi-Fi much of the time. I have unlimited talk and text, and then turn on data when I may need it for a trip. We really do not need data on our phones 24/7, but it has become normal. I am an Android OS phone user and do not have need or desire for the latest Apple product. I can replace my smartphone every 2 or 3 years, sell my old one phone on eBay, and only be out of pocket $100 or so. Consider all options and try to decide if you really need as much mobile data and services as you are paying for. There may be room for additional savings.

Home internet plans can be found in a variety of speeds and monthly data limits. We use one of the cheapest plans for our home internet. Some people can get by with only a mobile plan, but home internet data volume is usually less expensive than the same phone data volume. Public Wi-Fi can be found in many areas around town for those that opt to not pay for home internet via cable or DSL.

Many people have gym or fitness memberships, but we have opted to not do that. For exercise, we walk, bicycle, and take advantage of other free exercise options.

Clothing spending can consume significant resources. We personally avoid high priced labels and shop clearance racks in most stores. Many quality items can be found at used or consignment clothing stores, and a simpler wardrobe will keep expenses down. Finally, we do not shop just to pass time or for entertainment purposes. We shop when we have a need, and we try to clarify need versus want.

Less money can be spent on books and movies by borrowing them or shopping used bookstores. Movies and books can be borrowed at a public library. I try to avoid purchasing a book that I know I will only read once, opting instead to borrow or purchase used. Used books can also be found online at various websites for a fraction of the original sales price.

In our family, we try to be rational in our gift giving. Spending money on gifts can spiral out of control during the holidays, so we make a conscious effort to be smart and not try to compete with others. Be careful to not set expectations too high, which you might be tempted to increase year after year. We often opt for experiences and clutter-free gifts.

When we are shopping, we try to use a specific shopping list as often as we can. This helps us to avoid impulse buys and resist purchases that are not necessary. If I can avoid buying something on impulse, having extra time to think about the purchase will often help me to make a better decision or to not purchase an item that I really do not need.

Cleaning supplies can be made at home. There are options for creating basic cleaning products using simple ingredients that are less harsh and less expensive. Cleaners made with vinegar and baking soda and sometimes dish soap are quite common. A quick internet search will reveal many possible recipes.

The next suggestion has stirred some controversy in our household, but it has saved me hundreds of dollars over the years. I will often cut my own hair. I tend to keep my hair quite short, using a clipper cut length of 2 or 3. This is an easy task and is much faster than a trip and wait in the barber shop. My wife will occasionally urge me to 'let a professional' do it, but my own skill is good enough for my own satisfaction to get the job done for free. You may or may not be able to use this expense reduction, husbands beware.

A daily stop by a local coffee shop can add up to hundreds of dollars per year. We make our own coffee at home, even grinding whole beans with an inexpensive grinder. We may still get a coffee from a local place from time to time but making our own saves a significant amount of our resources, even if we buy quality beans or grounds.

Refurbished items can be a less expensive option for electronics and computers. I have purchased many computer systems and laptops as refurbished items. The warranty is often shorter, but I have not had a single issue with a refurbished item, and the savings can be significant. Other electronic items may be available as used or refurbished, but I usually opt for items from a source that includes a warranty, even if only 30 or 90 days.

Some items that break or fail can be fixed or repaired. This is not always possible, but when an item can be repaired, it reduces waste and saves money by avoiding a new purchase. Some household items can be glued, epoxied, sewed, or otherwise repaired and will often continue to work as good or better than before.

When travelling, one option to save money on a trip, especially if driving, is to pack food for one or more meals. We will often take a small cooler and pack food to make sandwiches at a roadside park or stop along the way. Even if we only do that for one meal for our family, it can save $20 to $40 versus eating at a restaurant. We will sometimes do this several times during our driving days, and it is convenient and simple.

Regarding life insurance, I only purchase term life. I consider life insurance as insurance, not an investment. I avoid whole life policies, as they are not a good investment in my opinion. Even with term life, once all our kids are out of the house, I will drop even that insurance and rely on savings if needed.

There may be subscriptions or memberships that are being paid for and not used. I would recommend that anyone periodically look over bank and credit card statements carefully for recurring payments. Evaluate whether these subscriptions are being used or needed. There may be memberships, services, plans, clubs, subscriptions, or other charges that can be eliminated without any noticeable impact.

As we downsized, we sold or donated many household items that we did not use or need. It reduced clutter and freed up space. Items were donated to Goodwill or other local causes, and some large items were sold locally or on Craigslist or Facebook.

Smaller items that can be mailed or shipped can be sold on eBay or other marketplace sites. We sold unneeded items such as tools, collections, books, movies, CDs, and used Amazon trade-in for some items. It was surprising how much money was raised and then saved by selling these unnecessary household items.

We review our overall budget status and spending annually or sometimes semi-annually. This annual review allows us to evaluate spending and expenses and decide if we want to change any of our financial habits. We can estimate a budget for the next year and look at ways to make possible changes. This process is quite helpful in our financial life.

An overall philosophy of owning less has helped our family reduce expenses. Less things mean less to store, repair, fix, maintain, etc. Owning less means that I purchase less, not that life is any less full or enjoyable. This philosophy has been freeing and lightened the burden of possessions. It has led to early retirement and the desire to write this book that might help others. Own less, live more.

Helpful Exercises

Look over the list of opportunities to reduce expenses above. Select five items that you want to consider to reduce expenses and increase savings.

1.
2.
3.
4.
5.

CHAPTER 12 - CONCLUSION

I have covered a large amount of material in an effort to offer as much helpful advice as possible. But these actions which worked well for me and my family and situation may not work for everyone. We all make our own choices in life and have different priorities. I urge you to choose carefully and choose well. Use the tips and information that helps and is beneficial to you. I am not a formally trained, paid expert, but my life experience has taught me many lessons.

To me, these are the most important and impactful topics to consider in our financial dealings:

Budget and track your expenses - It is extremely beneficial to know what we earn and what we spend. It is helpful to track expenses to be sure that we are not overspending. Budgeting helps us save money for future goals.

Separate financially related wants from needs - Our wants can tempt us to overspend and get us into financial trouble. Budgeting for needs and few of our wants will allow us to manage our finances more efficiently.

Choose your housing carefully, paying attention to size and cost - A larger home will commit us to larger fixed costs, including payments, taxes, insurances, maintenance, utilities, and more. This is an area where we should carefully consider our housing needs versus wants.

Avoid credit card debt - Interest rates are extremely high on credit cards. Minimum payments are such that it will take a long time to pay off a balance if only the minimum payment is made. Credit card debt can have a negative impact on our credit rating.

Pay off loans and debt early - We can save thousands of dollars in interest over the life of a loan if we pay extra principal and pay off a loan, mortgage, or debt earlier than scheduled.

Save and invest early and often - Saving early allows a longer time period and compounding interest to grow our savings and investments. Saving will provide an emergency fund and allow us to achieve future dreams and goals more easily.

Invest in index funds - Our investment strategy does not have to be complicated or placed into someone else's control. Choose stock and bond index funds for a long-term investment approach and reduce the stress and worry of watching the market fluctuations.

Life is a test, choose wisely. As Paul writes in Philippians 4, "I have learned the secret of being content in any and every situation, whether well fed or hungry, whether living in plenty or in want." Contentment is one of my personal goals. Contentment helps me to worry less about what others have and helps me to not buy things that I do not need.

Managing personal finances well can be a daunting task. I encourage you to start somewhere. Even small steps of progress will be helpful in your financial life. There is not a magic formula, and it will take effort. But the positive results of work and effort will pay more than just financial dividends in the future. I wish you well as you write your financial story.

* * *

[1] Wakefield, S. (2015). *Lightweight Bicycle Touring*. WakefieldSoft LLC.

[2] Wakefield, S. (2016). *A Father-Daughter Bicycle Touring Adventure*. WakefieldSoft LLC.

[3] Living Paycheck to Paycheck is a Way of Life for Majority of U.S. Workers, According to New CareerBuilder Survey. (2017, August 24). Retrieved from http://press.careerbuilder.com/2017-08-24-Living-Paycheck-to-Paycheck-is-a-Way-of-Life-for-Majority-of-U-S-Workers-According-to-New-CareerBuilder-Survey

[4] SPIVA: 2018 Active vs. Passive Scorecard. (2019, March 20). Retrieved from https://www.ifa.com/articles/despite_brief_reprieve_2018_spiva_report_reveals_active_funds_fail_dent_indexing_lead_-_works/

[5] Average credit card interest rates: Week of April 1, 2020. (2020, April 1). Retrieved from https://www.creditcards.com/credit-card-news/rate-report.php

[6] Consumer Credit Origination, Balance and Delinquency Trends: Q2 2019. (2019, August 23). Retrieved from https://www.transunion.com/blog/iir-consumer-credit-origination-q2-2019

[7] New US homes today are 1,000 square feet larger than in 1973 and living space per person has nearly doubled. (2016, June 5). Retrieved from https://www.aei.org/carpe-diem/new-us-homes-today-are-1000-square-feet-larger-than-in-1973-and-living-space-per-person-has-nearly-doubled/

[8] Leisure Time Physical Activity of Moderate to Vigorous Intensity and Mortality: A Large Pooled Cohort Analysis. (2012, November 6). Retrieved from https://journals.plos.org/plosmedicine/article?id=10.1371/journal.pmed.1001335

[9] Don't Eat Out as Often (188/365). (2017, October 18). Retrieved from https://www.thesimpledollar.com/save-money/dont-eat-out-as-often/

www.ingramcontent.com/pod-product-compliance
Lightning Source LLC
Chambersburg PA
CBHW050243220526
45465CB00002B/530